THROUGH
THE
DARK
WOODS

THROUGH
THE
DARK
WOODS

*A young woman's journey
out of depression*

Joanna Swinney

MONARCH
BOOKS

Oxford, UK & Grand Rapids, Michigan, USA

First published in the UK in 2006 by Monarch Books
(a publishing imprint of Lion Hudson plc),
Mayfield House, 256 Banbury Road, Oxford OX2 7DH.
Tel: +44 (0)1865 302750 Fax: +44 (0)1865 302757
Email: monarch@lionhudson.com
www.lionhudson.com

ISBN-13: 978-1-85424-768-1 (UK)
ISBN-10: 1-85424-768-9 (UK)
ISBN-13: 978-0-8254-6133-0 USA)
ISBN-10: 0-8254-6133-2 (USA)

Distributed by:
UK: Marston Book Services Ltd, PO Box 269,
Abingdon, Oxon OX14 4YN;
USA: Kregel Publications, PO Box 2607,
Grand Rapids, Michigan 49501

Unless otherwise stated, Scripture quotations are taken from the
Holy Bible, Today's New International Version, © 1973, 1978, 1984
by the International Bible Society. Used by permission of Hodder &
Stoughton Ltd. All rights reserved.

The text paper used in this book has been made from wood
independently certified as having come from sustainable forests.

British Library Cataloguing Data
A catalogue record for this book is available from the British Library.

Cover photo by Bruce Jeffrey
Cover illustration by Sandra Isaksson

Printed and bound in Great Britain by Cox & Wyman Ltd, Reading.

*Dedicated to my parents; with love
and gratitude for your
companionship on the journey
through the woods*

Contents

A Note About Who This Book is for

I have come to realise that depression is a widespread problem, and therefore the topic is relevant to a lot of us. My intended readership includes those who are currently depressed, those who used to be but no longer are, those who know someone who is or was depressed, those who are just interested in the subject, or those who know me and are reading it to be loyal even though they have no interest in depression at all! I have written it as a Christian, and some things will be more pertinent to those who are also Christians, but I hope it will have something to say to anyone, regardless of their spirituality or lack of it. So really, I have tried to cast the net pretty wide, and – whoever you are – please read, enjoy and join in the conversation.

Acknowledgments

I really need a whole other book for 'Thank Yous!' So many people have supported, encouraged and worked with me on this project. I have marvelled at times at my audacity to even attempt a feat such as this, and now I find myself at the point of completion I know it would not have been possible alone.

Thank you to Tony Collins at Monarch, for taking a risk with an unknown author and for being a fantastically encouraging and supportive editor. It has been a true pleasure to work with you. All the team at Monarch are wonderful – I landed on my feet with this publishing house: thank you guys!

I am grateful to Carolyn Armitage for her practical advice and encouragement when the manuscript was in foetal form. She gave me courage to go forward when it would have taken very little to stop me in my tracks.

Although the book has had the benefit of input from a huge number of people along the way, a handful have been particularly influential in the shape of the final product. I'd like to thank Becky Davies, Sophie Williams, Bekah Callow and my parents for the work and care they put into combing through the manuscript and giving me feedback. It is a much better book than it would have been without your comments. Thank you, thank you, thank you!

In addition to stories of my own life, I have drawn upon those of several people I know, and I am greatly indebted to those who have given me permission to do so. In particular, thank you to Gemma, Carolyn and Suzannah. Where permission has not been sought (and occasionally where it has), names and key details have been changed to protect identities.

Thank you to Charlie and Anita for letting me hunker down to write in their beautiful home in Oxford when I needed to get away from my messy house (I found I had no time to tidy or clean while writing). It was a great gift to have you close by – thank you for your loving hospitality and timely encouragement.

My family have been dispersed over three continents in the months I have been writing, but they have managed to stay closely involved. I love you all so much! Let's all get together soon, OK? Thank you Mum and Dad, Est and Rob, Jem and Davy and Bethie, for being the best family in the world *ever*!

Lastly, thank you to my Shawn. I am blessed indeed to share my life with you. Thank you for believing in me, smoothing my edges, keeping me going. I am yours forever xxx

Foreword

Jo is fun, she's serious, she's open yet protective of her own identity, she's an adventurer but doesn't forget where the safe places are, like a strong swimmer always with an eye on the beach. She writes engagingly and takes you to places that are familiar to every human being. Herein lies the importance of her story. Depressive feelings, as well as moments of elation, are the emotions of being alive and form the experience of us all, and clinical depression afflicts one in five of us. All of us will in our lifetime either experience depression or be affected intimately by someone who is depressed. This honest testimony of a young woman will help you identify and name these episodes and to know with a little more wisdom how to be and what to do when they happen.

These short chapters stand like sturdy stepping stones across a fast running river. You could jump quickly from one to the other and read the whole book in one sitting. But the real benefit is likely to come from dwelling on each stone, absorbing the scene and taking a look into the deep of the water. To do so will probably find you catching sight of your own reflection. This is where Jo's book will act like a mirror to your own life. Whether you see yourself as a depressive or the friend or the family of someone with depression you will get a glimpse of your own story and start reflecting on your moods, the reason why you feel the way you did and how you coped.

You may also hear in your own life the echoes of the man

from Nazareth who cried out 'My God, why have you abandoned me?'. These feelings of lonely forsakenness, so often the lot of the depressed, go right to the heart of God because they come right out of the heart of God! They were uttered by the Son of God as hung on dark wood. He cries out of the depths of his own being as he made his own journey through the dark woods. That's why he is such a sympathetic companion. As, indeed, is Jo.

The Rt. Revd James Jones
Bishop of Liverpool

A Fairy Tale

Once upon a time, in a land not so very far from here, there lived a little girl named Pearl. She was always smiley and happy for everyone treasured her, and she felt safe as could be in her cottage with her mother and father and flowers and birds all around.

This land had a wise and caring king, who often visited his citizens to make sure they were OK and sometimes stayed for tea and cake. He was such a good ruler that everyone trusted him to protect them from the dangers of the surrounding countries and even from the ones that lurked in the woods within their own borders. Pearl had known since she was a baby that the king was there to protect her.

One day, when Pearl woke up, she could feel that something was different. The first thing she noticed was that the sun was not shining through her red, checked curtains as it had done every morning that she could remember. And the fat, tortoiseshell cat that usually slept at the foot of her bed was not there. And now she realised that the smell of freshly baked bread and the sound of her mother singing were absent too. Things were definitely not as they should be. Still, Pearl decided not to panic, being mostly a sensible sort of person, and she got up and dressed and went downstairs.

After twice going through each room carefully, she realised she was alone in the cottage, which had never happened to her before and she was not sure at first what to do. Eventually she went outside, and called in case anyone was nearby. She called and called but there was no answer.

Now, I have told you how the citizens of this land trusted the king, and you must remember this or you will think what I am about to tell you very strange. For when after some time Pearl had accepted that she had been left all alone, and given the other things that were odd about the day, she decided to set out to the royal castle so the king could look after her until her parents returned and the sky went back to its usual sunny self (by now the clouds had grown extremely threatening).

She knew which way to go, because the king had built his castle on the tallest hill in sight. You could see it from anywhere in the land which made it very easy to find (I think that was why he chose to put it there, being as I said, very thoughtful).

Pearl set out feeling a little uneasy but mostly fine, because she had a plan, and she had packed some of yesterday's bread and a bottle of water. At first she made good progress, and even sang to herself for a while to cover up the silence, which was growing louder and louder as the day went on. But then she started to get scared. It seemed as though there were pairs of eyes peeping out at her from behind every tree, and sometimes she saw a shadow moving along beside her. In her haste to get to the king's castle she had not given a thought to the goblins and elves and creepy-crawly creatures that were said to live in the woods.

She went on for some time, walking faster and faster until she was quite out of breath and had to stop. She rested on a grassy patch and ate some of her bread and tried to cheer herself up by remembering all the things she liked in her cosy bedroom at home and how she would surely soon be back there with everything returned to normal. Once she felt better she got up to carry on. This was when the worst thing of all happened. She realised that for the first time in her life she could not see the hill with the castle on it! What was she to do? She started to run in panic, and as she ran the creatures of the woods ran too until they caught up with her and tore at her clothes and her hair and bruised her skin and scratched at her eyes. The sky grew darker still and great drops of rain fell amidst the sound of booming thunder. All was noise and confusion and pain and Pearl wondered if the end had come.

It was at this moment that Pearl, in the midst of her terror, became aware of another noise, a noise that had been there in the background all along. It was the sound of hooves, and it was growing louder. A great white horse galloped into sight, and on it rode the king. He swept her up onto the saddle and all the nasty beasts fell at the wayside. The sky was still dark and the rain still fell, but Pearl knew she was no longer alone and her heart gradually began to beat more slowly.

They arrived in due course at the castle and Pearl was wrapped up in a fine, soft blanket and given a large mug of creamy, hot chocolate. Although she was very relieved to have been rescued from the woods and was glad to be with the king, she still had many questions. The king listened patiently as she poured out her troubled heart. Where were her parents and why had she been left alone? Why had she not been able to see the castle when she needed to the most? Why had the sun gone behind the clouds and the rain fallen so hard on her?

When she had finished, the king lifted her onto his lap, for she was just a little girl, and he smiled sadly.

'I'm afraid I can't answer your questions my precious Pearl,' he said tenderly. 'But I can tell you that I was with you the whole time, and I always will be even when you can't see me, and you lose sight of my castle on the hill.'

Although this was not really a satisfactory answer in many ways, for some reason it was enough for Pearl at that moment, and she promptly fell asleep, worn out from the day's adventures.

Roots

I'd like to introduce myself. In choosing to write a book of this nature I feel as though I were sitting in some anonymous support group, declaring 'Hi, I'm Jo, and I'm a depressive' as though that were the word that most summed up my identity. It is not (at least, not most of the time). So, if you can, put aside that image and let me tell you about myself, before I delve into one particular aspect of my journey and convince you that I am a bleak and brooding person who likes nothing more than to curl up in a dark room with a box of tissues.

I was born in West Sussex in 1977, my parents' first child. We lived there until I was two when we moved to Bristol and lived in a top floor flat on Clifton Downs from which we could hear the zoo-lions roaring. We left Bristol with a sister for me (Esther) and a degree for Dad, allowing him to work as a curate in the Anglican Church.

Next stop for our small family was Upton, Merseyside, where we lived for three years. I started at the local primary school under the care of Mrs Turton. I also began to wear glasses. Mum and I tossed a coin about which frames I got – I wanted pink and she wanted tortoiseshell, the only options kindly offered free of charge by the National Health Service. She won, so I hid the ugly glasses in my school locker until I was found out and made to wear them. Jeremy, my brother, made his appearance sometime during the glasses saga. Estie and I had great fun dressing him up and doing his hair while he was small enough to be compliant (in fairness, I should add this was not for very long).

When I was five years old we moved to the Algarve, Portugal where my parents founded a Christian conservation project. It is now rather big and multi-national but in those days it was something of an extended family, based in a large, rambling farmhouse, 'Cruzinha'. Over time I became rather blasé about birds in the hand, reptiles in the freezer, and new faces at the dinner table, all of which bemused and bewildered the friends I occasionally brought home from school.

Bethan, my youngest sibling, was born in Lisbon when I was seven. We were all kept amused by her various eccentricities, including her early love of squid, gherkins, olives, and every available variety of fruit – she would occasionally disappear into the vineyard opposite Cruzinha, giving rise to mass searches, and in her case, a runny tummy.

I went to the International School of the Algarve until I was thirteen. Here I existed at the bottom of the social ladder, much derided and despised by all, until I left and was promptly forgotten. Bullying, as everyone knows, is very 'character building' so obviously I am thrilled to have gone through this experience! Thankfully I had a happy home life to balance it out: I have many memories of beach trips, barbequed chicken and chips in scruffy cafes, books read aloud, sailing our blue, Mirror dingy in the estuary, and a whole range of pets from guinea pigs and dogs to damaged birds of prey and carnivorous tadpoles, who unfortunately ate each other after being fed ham (NB don't feed tadpoles ham). No family is ideal but I never doubted I was loved and cherished, and this has been a great gift to me.

I was at boarding school in England for the last five years of my secondary schooling. None of us will ever forget the agony of the airport goodbyes, or the spine tingling ecstasy of the hellos. When I tell people about that experience I usually say the first year was hell, the second two were bearable and the last two were somewhat enjoyable. It is a deceptively easy summary of a complex chapter.

In my penultimate year at Dean Close my parents left Portugal, and were given a sabbatical, which took them to North and South America and the Middle East. Just over eighteen months later they settled in the south of France where they are still based. Meanwhile, I left school and spent a gap year in Zimbabwe. I began by teaching in a rural primary school and continued on with Scripture Union doing AIDS awareness in schools around Bulawayo. I went to Zimbabwe as the only Christian in our group and was quickly seduced by the apparent freedom to behave exactly as I chose, with no pressure from others' expectations or social conventions. The headiness soon turned to a feeling of emptiness. I had known God and was turning my back on Him for a series of rather shallow adventures. There came a crisis point, and I started to get back on track, with more support and no illusions about my own righteousness.

In September 1997 I started at Birmingham University reading English and African Studies. This did not make me very useful but I can talk books and have some views on the sociology of development, which comes in handy at dinner parties! More importantly perhaps, I made some wonderful friends, had lots of fun and did plenty of growing up.

After graduating I moved to Canada to study for a Master's in Christian Studies at Regent College in Vancouver. On Tuesdays we would have a chapel service. If I had to tell you one thing about Regent to give you an idea of what kind of a place it is, it would be that when we had communion we would have huge chunks of homemade bread dipped in pottery goblets of excellent wine. While I was there I met my husband Shawn, who is from Minneapolis, USA. After four years we moved to England to be closer to my family and are currently living in Buckinghamshire where Shawn is a youth pastor and I work as a keyworker at the National Society for Epilepsy.

Who Suffers From Depression?

In telling you the outline of my life so far I hope you will have got the impression (a truthful one) of someone who has had their ups and downs, but who has not undergone anything particularly unusual or nasty other than what anyone could expect living in a fallen world as a fallen person. And yet, I am someone who has experienced depression over a long period of time-years in fact. I have been a Christian with a real and vivid relationship with God my whole life. I have had a stable and loving family, I have never been without food or shelter. Am I unusual? No! Depression is unfortunately an extremely common affliction, dubbed 'the common cold of mental health' for the frequency of its occurrence. One in five people will experience depression at some stage during their life, so it might well affect you at some point, directly or indirectly.

Depression is not a condition limited to the emotionally challenged, the eccentric, the fringe lunatics. The club has had some prestigious members: Churchill (with his 'black dog'), Virginia Woolf, Henri Nouwen, Joni Mitchell, Vincent Van Gogh, the great preachers Luther, Spurgeon and Wesley...The list goes on and on, and includes many people who have contributed much to society in the midst of great suffering and struggle. A surprising number of history's great artists have been afflicted with depression, suggesting a mysterious connection on which many have speculated. There are even some very clear examples of depression amongst the Bible's great heroes: Elijah, Saul and David.[1]

What is It?

At the organic level, depression is a neurochemical disorder. I am not a bit scientific and have had to ask for explanations of this time and again. I will give it to you here as simply as I can (sorry if you are really clever and this sounds patronising). Basically, the brain is full of nerve cells talking to each other by sending electrical signals through a tiny gap called a synapse. In this gap there are lots of neurotransmitters, one of which is serotonin (there are others that are implicated in depression such as dopamine, but serotonin is the most common one). When a person is depressed, serotonin is used too much and so it gets depleted, and there isn't enough left of it to keep a proper balance going.

There are many kinds of mood disorders that fall into the 'depressive' category. Organic mood disorders are usually related to illness or drug side effects. Bipolar disorders include both depression and mania, a state in which the person may experience an elevated mood, or 'high', irritability, hyperactivity and other symptoms. Reading *The Wind in the Willows* recently, I had the revelation that Toad of Toad Hall is a classic example of someone with manic depression – one minute rushing around in a brand new motor car causing havoc, the next feeling miserable enough to die. Dysthemia is a low grade, long-term form of depression, and Major Depression is similar but more severe. Adjustment disorder involves symptoms that follow a major life change.[2] Seasonal Affected Disorder (SAD) is a relatively recently recognised condition that strikes hardest during winter.

Whilst I need to use the blanket term 'depression' for brevity, we must bear in mind the vast spectrum of illness that this word covers. John White, the late Christian psychiatrist and author of a number of books on this and other subjects, writes somewhat sternly that, 'Counsellors who try to help depressed people, and authors who write books about the subject, generally oversimplify the issue. Depression has many faces. It cannot be relieved on the basis of one simple formula, arising as it does by numerous and complex mechanisms, and plummeting sometimes to depths where its victims are beyond the reach of verbal communication. There are mysteries about it which remain unsolved. No one theoretical framework is adequate to describe it.'[3]

Physical illness is hard to bear, but I would venture to say that an illness of the mind can be an even greater suffering, as Peter C. Whybrow says, 'the illness enters and disturbs the person, that collection of feelings, behaviours, and beliefs that uniquely identify the human self. These afflictions invade and change the very core of being.'[4] I say that from the perspective of someone who has had depression but no major physical illness: if you have had both you would be in a better position to comment than I am.

Depression may involve some or all of the following symptoms: a depressed mood, an altered appetite leading to over or under eating, an inability to concentrate, insomnia or hypersomnia, thoughts of death, lack of interest in everyday activities, a sense of low self-esteem and guilt, a loss of energy and psychomotor retardation.[5] It is usually said that these symptoms must hang around for more than two weeks before they could amount to depression, but I know from personal experience that a day or two can be wretched enough to warrant the title.

We must also be clear about what depression is not. It is hard to explain to someone who has not experienced the transition over that fine line of normality. Depression is completely distinct from common or garden emotional distress: just as once you've had flu you would never confuse it with a cold, even a really bad one, so depression is entirely different from a regular low mood, experienced by all of us in the normal course of events.

Where Does It Come From?

The causes of depression are many and various. Some have an unfortunate genetic disposition to the illness, and inherit an innate tendency towards succumbing to it. It may take very little, if anything, to throw such a person into the depths of despair.

Depression can be the body's response to a trauma: bereavement, unemployment, financial stress, an accident or a major life change, even one that is to all intents and purposes positive, such as marriage, a promotion or a new baby. All these changes are intensely disruptive, and can throw our emotional equilibrium completely out of kilter.

Physical illness can be a precipitator: I spent two weeks weeping my way through a bout of flu last year, feeling enormously sorry for myself, only to perk up with the return of my health and energy. For people who go through major sickness, depression can be a response to the loss of independence and dreams for the future, as well as the exhaustion of living with constant pain. It can be a side effect of drugs administered to treat the sickness, or other medications such as the contraceptive pill.

It is far more common for women to become depressed, as we have the hormonal storms to ride around puberty, childbearing and the menopause. Ten per cent of women world-wide experience post-natal depression.[6] We are also more likely to internalise anger, pushing it in and down until it becomes something more menacing altogether. Men do experience depression too, but may be more likely to become violent or find escape in alcohol or drugs. They might find themselves depressed by the inability to fulfil their ambitions, by a perceived lack of status or success, or by unresolved conflict.

While depression has been around from time immemorial, it seems to have reached epidemic proportions in our era and culture, and perhaps especially so amongst my generation. I tend to think this makes sense. We grow up being told that the possibilities are endless and that we will be able to do anything we set our minds to. This sets up impossibly high expectations, as well as a hefty responsibility to make something of our lives. Reality hits hard, and the disillusionment is bitter. Our society is highly individualistic and interpersonal commitment is low, so we feel essentially alone in the world. Isolation and loneliness are widespread. In my lifetime there have been countless natural and man-made disasters, the tsunami of 2004, the terrorist attacks perpetrated by al-Qaeda around the world, the genocide in Rwanda in 1994, and many others. We are close to these events through media and travel and they leave a deep sense of insecurity, sadness and helplessness. Our planet has been trashed and we are already seeing the effects in water shortages, extreme weather and increases in environmentally caused disease such as skin cancer. We lack many of the certainties of previous ages: it seems that everything is up for grabs from the meaning of life to the existence of God. Existential angst is rife. All of these aspects of modern living could contribute towards a tendency to be depressed.

There are some who would say that depression is a result of sin in a person's life. Could this be the case? John White sees a definite connection, both direct and indirect. Indirectly, sin is the cause of all suffering through the fall, since which the whole of creation has been groaning, as in the pangs of childbirth (Romans 8: 19–22).

Directly, depression may follow as a result of sinful choices we have made, decisions to turn our backs on God in deliberate disobedience. It can be a consequence of living a life we know to be inconsistent with our inner values and beliefs. White explores the idea that, 'a wrong relation with God exposes us to the risk of insanity, and a right relation with God is a move in the direction of mental health. After all,' he continues, 'if God designed us to be related to him, what would be more natural?'[7] This is a complex and charged subject, and I don't want to dismiss it immediately out of hand, as I really do think sin can play a part in depression. However, to attribute depression to sin is a dangerous move and needs greater wisdom and spiritual sensitivity than most of us possess. Proceed with caution down this route, or don't proceed at all.

With the benefit of hindsight and several years of counselling, I would say that my own depression had several causes. I believe I have a genetic disposition, and am temperamentally prone to it, being someone who naturally hits life's highs and lows with full force. I started boarding school at an age when most people are an emotional shambles anyway, and homesickness, bullying and bad weather all added to the pressure. As a volatile person, I sometimes found it hard finding an appropriate vent for anger growing up in a fairly public family, with parents who place a high value on harmony and politeness. I found it hard to leave Portugal and struggled to feel 'at home' anywhere for a few years afterwards. I got involved in several intense romantic relationships and then crashed when they ended. I could go on but I think I could quickly begin to sound whiney and self-pitying... forbid the thought!

Digging for the roots of your depression can be productive, if it enables you to move on and grow in self-understanding. However, it can be a dangerous pursuit. You may want to beware of the following:

1. Becoming self absorbed and inward looking. Taking yourself too seriously, and over dramatising your life. We all have our wounds. We are all broken.
2. Blaming everyone else for how you turned out. No one has perfect parents (some have none at all), perfect friends, perfect teachers. We are not dealt equal cards. We must take responsibility for ourselves and how we turn out.
3. Losing yourself in the past and forgetting the pressing issues of the present and future that need your attention more urgently.

At the end of the day, as Elizabeth Wurtzel has said, perhaps 'the particulars of what has driven this or that person to

Zolft, Paxil, or Prozac, or the reasons that some other person believes herself to be suffering from a major depression, seem less significant than the simple fact of it.'[8] What we are left with is the question of how to deal with it.

Chapter 2

Dragons

I want to share something of what depression has been like for me with two aims: the first, to try to describe as best I can what it feels like for those of you who have not gone through it, so you can maybe get some insight and therefore hopefully increased patience and compassion for those who suffer from it. I realise there is some inherent futility to this exercise. William Styron put it this way: 'Depression is a disorder of mood, so mysteriously painful and elusive in the way it becomes known to the self – to the mediating intellect – as to verge close to being beyond description. It thus remains nearly incomprehensible to those who have not experienced it in its extreme mode...'[1] While it may be incomprehensible, I still think it is worth trying to understand. I have always processed my experiences verbally and find it helpful at least to attempt to put things into words. If those you know are unable to do this, I hope my offering might be helpful.

My second aim is to offer solidarity to those who are or have been depressed – you are not alone in what you are going through. There is a strange coherence to the descriptions of depression that people give. As T.S Eliot's character Sir Henry Harcourt-Reilly says in *The Cocktail Party*, 'All cases are unique, and very similar to others.'[2] Dorothy Rowe, a world-renowned clinical psychologist, who has spent many years devoted to researching depression, has found that people's images of depression are consistently one of the following: the person surrounded in thick fog, lost and hopeless; the person stranded in an empty landscape, either a desert, an ocean or a wasteland of some kind; images of a person in space, crushed or tightly wrapped in some restrictive garment; the person trapped in a tunnel, pit or cage. All these images have a common thread: a terrible sense of isolation.[3] There is of course an irony in this: although you feel as though no one could ever understand what you're going through, many people are going through the exact same thing.

The Dragon Comes Out of its Lair

I'm pretty sure my first major episode of depression was when I started at boarding school in England at the age of thirteen. Thirteen is generally a difficult age anyway, what with spots, unruly hormones and the uneasy coexistence of child and nascent adult in the same body. This dangerously explosive primordial slime cocktail of personhood that I was at the time was ensconced in a crowded dormitory of equally unstable thirteen-year-old girls and perhaps the emotional shipwreck that followed was inevitable.

It is hard to pinpoint when exactly you have left the realm of the 'normal' spectrum of emotion and arrived in the land of depression. It has a way of creeping up on you. You have a bad day, then another one, then you realise it has been three weeks since you had a good day, then you can't remember what a good day feels like, and you realise that BAM! you're depressed and goodness knows when it happened. Andrew Solomon talks about depression being both a birth and a death, involving both a new presence and an absence. He goes on to say:

> *Birth and death are gradual, though official documents may try to pinion natural law by creating categories such as 'legally dead' and 'time born'. Despite nature's vagaries, there is definitely a point at which a baby who has not been in the world is in it, and a point at which a pensioner who has been in the world is no*

longer in it. It's true that at one stage the baby's head is here and
his body is not; that until the umbilical cord is severed the child
is physically connected to the mother. It's true that the pensioner
may close his eyes for the last time some hours before he dies,
and that there is a gap between when he stops breathing and
when he is declared 'brain-dead' Depression exists in time. A
patient may say that he has spent certain months suffering
major depression but this is a way of imposing a measurement
on the immeasurable. All that one can really say for certain is
that one has known major depression, and that one does or does
not happen to be experiencing it at any given moment.[4]

I certainly remember the start of the slide this particular
time. On Saturdays The Institution had decreed the inmates
were allowed to wear clothes from home, termed 'mufti' as in
the similarly regimented army context. This was essentially
a good thing, as our uniform consisted of a maroon skirt,
maroon and white tie, maroon v-neck sweater and knee
length maroon socks held up by grey elastic garters. The first
Saturday arrived, and I blithely donned my pale blue jeans,
tight around my ankles, baggy sweatshirt and worst of all,
white socks inside my black shoes. A gaggle of girls drew
around me to point out my dreadful mistakes, moving on to
let me know that I would have to grow my fringe out (no one
has a fringe) and that my nose spoiled any chance I had of
being pretty. Having given their pronouncement, they moved
away to continue dressing in their own, acceptable
garments, and brushing their uniformly long hair, leaving me
bewildered (who cares what colour socks are? Are these girls
mad?) and unsure of myself. This was the start of it all.

It became apparent that of the ten of us in our dorm there
were three friendship groups of three, with the one left over
being yours truly. It was a familiar scenario. I had spent the
break times at my school in Portugal trailing around the
edge of the playground hoping to be noticed and ignored in

equal, painful measure. Here I was again, and it seemed like all the confirmation I needed to believe that I was fundamentally flawed and belonged on the outside. I began to feel desperately miserable. Around this time I wrote the following in a letter to my parents: *'I guess it's going well, but I'm quite lonely. It's just things like no one to sit next to in lessons, being left behind in lunch and not having a partner in P.E. It seems history repeats itself. Once more I'm forced to be a loner and I hate it.'*

While the school in Portugal had been perhaps equally dreadful, I was able to go home at the end of the day and be reminded of the bigger picture. Here I was stuck, and as the days went by I completely lost any reference points outside my situation. I struggled to remember anything about my home or family, or even who I had been before I arrived here.

Initially my feelings were attached to objective facts about my situation, all of which seemed rational. 1. I was homesick. 2. The girls in my dorm were being horrid, as only teenage girls know how. 3. England was bleak and grey and dark, whereas Portugal was sunny and vibrant with colour. However, gradually my misery became its own being, with a life that needed no reasons to exist. It sat in my tummy and made me feel like I had eaten rocks. It wrapped itself around my chest and made it hard to breathe. It jumped up and down on my head poking its fingers around in my brain, making me confused. It puffed itself up like a cloud and obscured the light. It came everywhere with me, and it stopped people from seeing who I was. Mum wrote this to me with great wisdom and insight: *'You must fight your feelings of depression Jo. They allow you to believe things about yourself and life and God that are not true, they damage your faith and trust in God and make them melt away like snow on a sunny day – and they damage you and make it very difficult for people to come close to you. Resist the temptation to get locked up inside yourself...'* Fighting and resisting came much later though. For a while I was defeated.

Anatomy of a Dragon

The internal and external realities of depression are poles apart. From the outside, that first term at boarding school, I was a quiet, tearful, introverted schoolgirl. I made it to my lessons on time, I did my homework, mostly I ate regularly (there was only one week when I couldn't get food down). I had dark circles under my eyes and rarely smiled, but really there was nothing major to indicate what was happening internally. On one occasion I missed a sports session as I was sobbing on the shoulder of a sympathetic sixth former, and a few of the more dramatic girls in my year were convinced I had gone off to kill myself (this was probably more a reflection of their guilty consciences than any real sense of danger that I would actually put an end to my life). Other than that, things ticked along pretty uneventfully. Because I was functioning normally, I was left to my own devices to cope. I remember reaching out for help a couple of times, once to the school chaplain, and again to my Godfather when he came to visit. The school chaplain seemed impervious, stone deaf, to my plea for rescue. I found out afterwards that my Godfather really had grasped the severity of my inner situation. At the time though, I felt that no one had any ability to help. Elizabeth Wurtzel writes in *Prozac Nation*, 'If you're still at the point when you're even just barely going through the motions – showing up at work, paying the bills – you are still OK, or OK enough. A desire not to acknowledge depression in ourselves or those close to us- better known these days as denial, is such a strong urge that plenty of people prefer to think that until you are actually flying out of a window, you don't have a problem.'[5]

Part of the subjective experience of depression is intense isolation. Maybe my sense of abandonment was inaccurate, but it is how I remember that time. I felt myself to be achingly alone. Sounds might have come out of my mouth but they were lost in the airwaves. Kind hands might have reached towards me, but I never felt their touch. I had retreated deep inside myself, beyond the range of human comfort.

Even now, recollecting in tranquillity, as Wordsworth was so fond of doing, I cannot come close to putting words to what I went through at that time. Words would contain the uncontainable, categorise and simplify what was pure chaos. I could say I felt fearful, panicked, lost, alone, hopeless, trapped, sad, exhausted...all of which would be true, but still would not capture it. Most days there would be a moment of surrender, when I would find a private space to lie down and wait for the world to end. It is hard to find such a place in a boarding school, so I would often resort to the girls' PE changing room – smelly, damp and bleak – a suitably awful setting perhaps! There would be momentary relief as the tears I had held back during lessons were able to stream out, but then I would realise with horror that I had no good reason to pull myself together. But somehow, time and time again, the tears would abate and I would wash my face and rejoin the maroon-clad hordes as unobtrusively as possible.

When I went home to Portugal that Christmas I was a sorry puddle of a person. To be embraced by the love of my mum and dad, lap up the warmth of the fire and my reassuring bedroom, participate in the festivities of the season, only served to increase my dread at the thought of having to go back to school. I had thought that being at home would give me a magical lift, but it took a lot more than that.

It was several months later that I started to realise I didn't feel quite so desperate any more. Occasionally I even had days when I felt something akin to happiness, when I realised I was enjoying something, experiencing pleasure, laughing. Whybrow describes the process of recovery in a way that I can relate to perfectly:

[It is] like coming out of a dream where you have distorted all sorts of things but in waking up you forget the distortions...People can look at you and tell the difference. It's in the face - the smile lines return - and you start to talk faster. Actually, as you become reacquainted with yourself, other people confirm that because they start talking to you again, almost as if nothing had happened.[6]

The next few years, until I left school, did not have any times approaching the misery of my first term. There were many seasons, however, that I would realise that I had felt somehow down, grey, unhappy for the previous few weeks, and that I was only getting worse. I would long to be lying in bed, buried beneath the covers. When the alarm woke me each morning my first awareness would be a heavy, sinking sensation in the pit of my stomach. My thoughts would be negative and circular, one thought leading to the next like links in a chain wrapping its way around me and trapping me with despair. I would have to put more energy into functioning normally than the average person. It all seemed such an appalling effort.

Dragons Don't Make Good Pets

A brief survey of the years after I left school, up until I was 25 and began to turn a significant corner towards recovery, reveals four more periods of 'major depression', and long-term dysthymia, a lower grade depression, that believe it or not is still not much fun! Each time I became low I would drearily think to myself, this is just how it is. This is who I am and how my life feels. When I felt OK I always had a sense it couldn't last, the floorboards just weren't very strong or secure beneath my feet. I could pretty much guarantee that any challenge that came my way would poleaxe me for several months, very quickly drawing in a host of other issues like a train with many carriages. For example, when I broke up with a boyfriend at university, I was soon battling with self-esteem (I am a hideous troll), fear of the future (I will live in a bed-sit with no heating or furniture and count all the white cars going by to pass the lonely hours), past failures (not being chosen as a school prefect, forgetting to feed my pet rabbits, not being Mary in a nativity play ever and on and on) until the break-up was the least of my worries.

I often battled with deep anxiety about the future, burdened by a sense that my life's progress was in my own hands and convinced that I would let it slip through my fingers, wasting opportunities and failing at every turn to make a success of myself. I remember walking around Selly Oak on a sunny afternoon with my parents who had come to visit during my second year of university. I was trying to explain to them how bleak my prospects were, and how much I dreaded graduating and having to face THE NEXT STEP. They seemed truly baffled, because as my loyal progenitors they believed in me, and saw my future in far brighter terms. It was as though we were looking at the same painting through different coloured glasses, completely altering its appearance.

Dragons Smell Fear

In a sense, I learned to live with my dragons, adapting to life with them and doing my best to keep them quiet and well behaved. I was always aware of them, feeling their fiery breath on my back, their ugly, scaly presence at my side. I wondered if one day they would turn on me and gobble me up for good. I didn't know what this would look like exactly (in the terms of the metaphor, probably a pulpy, bloody mess) – maybe madness or death. I was never hospitalised, as many are, and I never had a full-blown breakdown, as many do. For this I can only thank God.

As I write, it has been three years since I have been properly depressed. I have had bad days, weeks even, but never bad enough to compare to depression as I have known it in the past. The thing is though, I panic when I get down because the memory of how it feels is so vividly clear in my mind. It has become the fear of a fear. I really, REALLY don't want to wake the dragons up from their slumber.

So that's how we stand. I hope my experience hasn't been too depressing for you to read. Maybe you should take a break and read some Calvin and Hobbes – the cartoon, not the two authors – for a bit to cheer yourself up. See you next chapter.

Chapter 3

Stigma

'A mark or sign of disgrace or discredit' (Oxford English Dictionary)

When I told people I was writing a book, I received blanket approval and affirmation. When I told them what it was about, it was a different story. Here are some of the responses I got:

'Don't expect me to put it on my coffee table!'
'What a depressing topic. Heh heh!' (I got quite a few variations on this joke.)
'Oh. How's work these days?' (A desperate attempt to change the subject.)
'Who's going to want to read a book on depression?'
'Now why would you choose to write about something like that?' (In response to my reply that it comes out of personal experience the person would look at me like I had just picked my nose in front of them.)

A survey carried out into the public perception of the causes of depression found that 71 per cent felt it was due to emotional weakness, 45 per cent that it was the victim's fault, and 35 per cent that it was due to 'sinful behaviour'.[1] All I can say to that is: 'Yikes!' (my favourite word at the moment). As a condition, depression is more disabling than any other disorder with the exception of advanced coronary heart disease.[2] It affects sleep, appetite, esteem, energy, sexuality and the ability to concentrate and perform tasks. It involves psychological, social and spiritual factors, but is also biological in nature (sometimes entirely biological). And yet, it is surrounded by a stigma that leaves sufferers feeling guilty and ashamed, fearful of confessing their condition and even of getting treatment. Whybrow argues that it is only recently that mood disorders have been seen as an illness requiring medical attention, and that with the exception of the Greek and Roman eras, 'Western society has been more inclined to condemn than to cure when confronted with manic and depressive disability.'[3]

Shortly before Shawn and I moved to England I mentioned to a friend that I would like to start a support group for people with depression in our church. I was surprised and taken aback when he impressed upon me his concern that I keep my own depression quiet in order to avoid the judgment and mistrust he felt I would face as a result. His fear was that in a culture of success and achievement I would be branded as a failure.

Not long after, in applying for my job at the National Society for Epilepsy, I was obliged to complete a medical form that asked me whether I had ever been treated for depression. I was on antidepressants, and as a result I was sent to the occupational health department at the local hospital to be assessed for competency. Whilst I understand that depression might have compromised my ability to perform in the workplace, I was not asked if I had depression, only if I was currently on medication. I confess the whole process made me feel extremely vulnerable about having sought help: it seemed to have made me a more dubious prospect as an employee.

Cultural Stigma

I suspect there is more stigma around depression in England than in some other countries. Generalisations are always very limited but here are my home-brewed observations of the British. As a nation we have a reputation for keeping unseemly displays of emotion under wraps, being part of a 'cult of the stiff upper lip'.[4] We do not like to take ourselves too seriously and we do not like to introspect, to 'navel-gaze'. We are generally private and like our space, hence the old cliché, 'an Englishman's home is his castle'. It goes against the grain to reach out for help, be it to friends or professionals. My grandparents were English to the core. Once when my mother was upset after sending us off to school for the term, my grandmother said to her rather briskly, 'They're not dead, dear!' I couldn't imagine trying to explain my depression to her especially with so much going for me on the surface of things.

Just the other day I was listening to a London talk radio station, where the subject of the call-in was depression. The gist of most of the callers and even the host himself was that most people claiming to be depressed are fakers who take themselves too seriously and are looking for excuses to stay home from work. Whybrow states that 'It is a commonly held sentiment in our society that depression is moral weakness. It is in our belief system and at the root of the shame and stigma that many who suffer depression still bear.'[5]

Depression is a form of mental illness, and mental illness makes people afraid. It originates in that most mysterious of organs, the brain, about which there is still so much to learn. Before the earth's surface had been fully explored, cartographers would fill in the empty spaces with fantastical beasts and fearsome landscapes, sometimes writing the ominous phrase, 'here be dragons'. The unknown is always feared.

Stigma from Christians

Sadly, in some parts of the church there is just as much stigma around depression as in wider society, and this can be even harder to break down as it is rooted in a form of spirituality. There are Christians who truly believe that mental illness is largely a result of 'insufficient faith, inadequate commitment, personal sin or disobedience to God'.[6]

I have encountered this attitude many times myself. On one particular occasion, when I was a student, I went to church feeling as vulnerable as a peeled, hard-boiled egg, deep in depression and misery. I tried to bolt at the end of the service, before the milling around bit got underway, but before I got to the door I was collared by a well-meaning, very kind, elderly lady. On seeing the state I was in, she whipped me back in a pew and had me trawling through my wrong-doings, thoughts, words and deeds, so I could repent and thus feel all better. Needless to say, I did not feel better, but rather significantly worse.

A few weeks ago I bumped into a Christian friend on the high street. We got talking about her son, Jon, who is at university in his first term. To her great distress he has become withdrawn and miserable. He feels he is incapable of doing his work and has not made friends. He has been advised by his personal tutor to go on antidepressants and seek counselling but his mother feels strongly that to do this would be wrong, would contradict his faith, and hers. She just knows that if he would only pray more and make some Christian friends, that he would snap out of it and be fine. He is obviously not walking closely enough with God. She is a loving and committed mother, but I fear she is doing her son a great disservice by holding these views, and by doing her best to prevent him seeking any form of 'non-spiritual' help. I do not wish to preclude the fact that God can step in and lift depression, much as he can heal a person of cancer or mend a broken bone. However, he does not always work in this way, any more with brokenness of the mind than of the body. It can be easy to over-spiritualise depression which hinders rather than helps the process of healing. Many times

I have felt guilty for feeling the same way after a long session of prayer, attempting to release my anxiety to God ('casting my cares on him') and repenting for any sin in my life.

Combating Stigma

Being aware of the stigma can create a sense of shame about any association with depression: it is shared as a guilty secret, whispered about furtively in corners or rushed over with platitudes. In the course of writing this book, I had to tell many people I didn't necessarily know well about the personal nature of the story. I found I had to battle the vulnerability of knowing that the revelation could mean I had lowered myself in people's estimation. I could not predict how they would respond and unfortunately I still care far too much about what people think of me: I am very much a work in progress.

Combating stigma means combating prejudice, which stems from ignorance. Dealing with ignorance is a question of education. We must be willing to (gently) confront attitudes that stem from ignorance, and teach people what this is all about. Before we can do that though, we must look at any stigma we ourselves attach to depression. I know I have had to do a lot of undoing in my own thinking on this. If we are embarrassed or ashamed to admit what we are going through, we will only compound the problem.

In the grand scheme of things, I have encountered the stigma attached to mental health in a very minor way. Stigma is a harsh reality for many in our world, and if we get a small taste of it in our own lives, it might help us to confront any prejudice we harbour and become a little more tolerant and compassionate towards those who suffer from conditions we know nothing about.

Chapter 4

Naming

What's in a name? A rose by any other name would smell the same after all, wouldn't it? Does the word we allocate to something or someone actually matter? The complexity of this subject makes my mind hurt. Over time I have come to believe that yes, semantics are important, terribly important, because of the way that they carry and even create meaning. Political correctness has its vehement critics, and has spawned some very amusing satire (See for example James Finn Garner's book, *Politically Correct Bedtime Stories*[1]). I have been around dinner tables where anecdotes of the madness of this drive to change language have been bandied about with great hilarity.

But think of how our use of language around those with disabilities has changed the way we perceive them. It is no longer acceptable to call someone a 'spastic', a 'retard' or a 'loony'. Apart from the fact that this defines their whole personhood by one aspect of what makes them up, these words are powerfully demeaning and degrading. By the same token, at the National Society for Epilepsy, where I work, we are all careful to refer to 'people with epilepsy' rather than to 'epileptics', a small but weighty distinction.

Solomon writes that, 'most psychodynamic therapies are based on the principle that naming something is a good way to subdue it.'[2] In Genesis, once God had created something he named it: 'And God said, "Let there be light," and there was light. God saw that the light was good, and he separated the light from the darkness. God called the light "day", and the darkness he called "night" (Genesis 1:3–5). When Adam was given dominion over the animals by God, we immediately see him naming them, apparently to God's approval as God himself takes up the names! Naming in ancient times denoted ownership or authority over something or someone.[3]

How is a Diagnosis Reached?

Hippocrates is considered the father of modern medicine. It was he who first articulated the importance of observing disease over time, taking careful note of clinical details in what we would now call a case history. It was Hippocrates who first saw the link between brain injuries and the convulsive fits that his contemporaries understood to be a visitation from the gods.

Diagnosis is essentially scientific classification, based upon current and historical observation. Ideally it will not only describe and characterise, but will provide a prediction of the outcome of events. This is a far more complex matter when it comes to illness of the mind rather than the body:

> Losing control of the arms and legs is very different from loss of control of thinking, or how we feel emotionally. Objective classification of the body and its organs is a simple business compared to that of classifying mind, mood and emotion – the complexities of the private self.'[4]

There is a clustering of symptoms around depression, such as anxiety, sleep disturbance and loss of energy, and it is commonly agreed upon that for a reliable diagnosis of depression to be made, at least five of these symptoms will be present over a period that exceeds two weeks. At present there is no laboratory test that can prove the diagnosis beyond doubt, so doctors rely on observations and historical evidence.

Euphemisms

Over the years I have developed various ways of referring to my depression: 'the dreads', 'the dragons', 'feeling low'. Other euphemisms include 'the blues' or 'the darkness'. These terms were a way of referring to what I struggled with without giving it a label. It was important to me, my friends and my family to avoid the particular label of depression. I think all of us feared the implications: for me, the idea that I would be branded by society as someone who couldn't cope, that I would be passed by for opportunities and relationships as though infected with a gloomy plague; for my loving and committed and involved parents, the spectre of responsibility rose before them and a nagging worry that a tidy diagnosis might release me from the necessity of being accountable for myself and my life, so becoming the self-pitying victim of a condition I had no control over. While it was 'the dragons' I could take up my sword and fight an honourable battle to the death (hopefully of the dragons not of me). Dragons were comfortably external. Mum and I would often finish phone conversations with a rallying cry of 'slay the dragons!' and I would put down the receiver with a vivid picture of a little green creature with a spiky spine and goggle eyes meekly lying down to die. Hoorah!

In my second year at university, the dragons got me once again. During this particular episode I went to stay with some close family friends up in Liverpool. Vicky is a psychologist, and together we sat down for a focused discussion on the Saturday morning. I described to her how I had been feeling, the way I was waking up early in the morning unable to get out of bed for fear of what the day would hold, the way that everything felt overwhelming and dark. She listened intently, becoming the professional I had only known she was in theory, and after some probing questions pronounced that it sounded to her like 'casebook depression'. I remember weeping with a strange relief – my suspicions that what I had been dealing with was not in a healthy emotional spectrum had at last been validated and I felt my sufferings, meagre as they were, had been taken seriously. While there would be plenty of dark times to come, I see that as a pivotal moment in the process of recovery. As long as it remained an amorphous threatening cloud it was not treatable, did not merit treatment. As 'depression' it could be categorised and ambushed with all the combined expertise of medicine and psychology until it cowered in submission. I did not have to struggle on alone, working at my strategics, because I knew there were many, many others who experienced the same thing and that there was some biochemical reason for it.

But on the Other Hand...

When I first landed my diagnosis, it was a great gift. But it soon became apparent that the gift had its issues to be negotiated. It was tempting to sink into it and give up struggling – I had depression, a medical condition, so I shouldn't be expected to be operating at par. Whereas before I had done my utmost to continue life as usual, I became more likely to take to my bed and mope: I had a chemical imbalance in my brain, so what else could be expected of me? I think I began to take myself and my problems rather seriously. Later, once I had begun official counselling, as I raised whatever new and important tragedy I had uncovered in my life, my psychiatrist would gently remind me that it was really rather normal to dislike criticism/ hate my job/ have days I felt fat and ugly/ worry about money...it wasn't all down to chemicals and I retained my responsibility for dealing with my life and its pedestrian concerns.

In my job I often see people have their diagnosis of epilepsy taken from them and replaced with the frustratingly vague diagnosis of 'Non-Epileptic Attack Disorder'. Although this means they can come off their potent pills and have a greater chance of becoming seizure-free in time, this change is a traumatic one. Their diagnosis has become who they are – has defined and changed their lives - and they desperately resist having it taken from them, even if the alternative is to all intents and purposes better for them. They have an identity that has become intrinsically rooted in the disorder they thought they had.

Hopefully, we take our diagnosis as a means to an end – a way of locating the kind of approach we should take to eradicate the condition. A diagnosis should never define us, or become us. We are all far more than the sum of our medical conditions; we are multidimensional rainbows of character, history, and context. Sue Atkinson, author of *Climbing Out of Depression* had a rough ride in her road to diagnosis, and in the midst of it felt that her humanity was overlooked:

> *What gave me my first insight into the idea that doctors and psychiatrists might not always be right with their labels was that each one I saw gave me a different one... Not only was that really mind-blowingly funny, it was utterly disconcerting. I didn't see myself as a 'cyclic depressive with paranoid tendencies'. I was a hurting person and I wanted to know why.*[5]

A diagnosis, a name, is a helpful tool, but we must be careful to keep it in its proper perspective. It can enable us to recognise what it is we are dealing with, and how best to treat it, but it should never be allowed to dictate who a person is. If we are avoiding an official title for a condition, we should look carefully at why. It could be a function of our pride or fear.

Chapter 5

Support

During our first year back in England, Shawn and I had a friend move in with us for a couple of months. We liked thinking of ourselves as providing a refuge for those who needed one, and here was a chance to put this into practice while gaining some treasure in heaven and kudos on earth. It seemed like a win-win situation. Laurel was funny, vivacious and articulate. I had always enjoyed her company and wanted to see more of her. I had missed her during my four years in Canada. Our house was small, narrow and three stories tall, but we had the luxury of a second bedroom, and she had nowhere to go.

So Laurel and her depression came to stay. And we soon realised her depression was more of a presence than Laurel herself. It was a wake-up call. There were moments I wanted to shake her: I got frustrated at how much mess she made and her erratic habits. We repeatedly had the same conversations, as though we were reading from a dog-eared script that both of us had tired of but couldn't put down. She cried incessantly, didn't shower very often, and wallowed in the bleakness of her situation over one too many glasses of red wine. I started to dread coming back from work because our home seemed to smell of depression. It lingered in the air like poisonous gas. When she left we felt guilty relief, as well as a degree of exhaustion.

I tell that story with a sense of shame, wishing that my patience and compassion had been wider and deeper, and that I was more like Jesus. It shocked me to the core to realise how conditional my acceptance of Laurel was, and how short I fell of my own ideals of friendship. Reflecting on the experience in the months that followed, I tried to untangle my confused responses. I realised I was afraid she would pull me into her mood – I carried her and her struggles around with me in my thoughts and my prayers, and it felt too heavy a load. I had been occupied with my own life and concerns and her needs impinged on my freedom. I wondered if I was looking into a mirror and seeing a reflection of myself in my depressed times, and what I saw scared me. If I was growing tired of her, surely people had grown tired of me in the very same way? It was a deeply uncomfortable revelation. I needed my ministrations to make a difference; to make her, even just a little, better. When my efforts didn't pay off I ran out of patience, far sooner than I care to admit. Living with her and with my responses to her was a constant, grating reminder of my limitations, and the chasm between my idealistic notions of myself as a sacrificial, compassionate, loving person and the narky, short-tempered, uncaring reality. I wanted to be the sort of person who could help – especially as I of all people should have known what she was going through.

Hang In There – It's Not Easy

Have you resonated at all with that sorry tale? I want you to know that if you struggle to like, let alone love, your depressed friend/spouse/family member, that is perfectly understandable. Let no one underestimate the cost of love in these circumstances – it is a very great gift and comes at a high price to the giver. It is hard and painful and it takes courage to support someone with depression. As Sheila Cassidy, a woman with intimate knowledge of suffering, writes, 'He who would be a companion to the dying [or depressed]...must enter into their darkness, go with them at least part way along their lonely and frightening road. This is the meaning of compassion: to enter into the suffering of another, to share in some small way in their pain, confusion and desolation.'[1]

To enter into someone else's suffering means taking leave of your comfort, and walking deliberately into pain that is not your own. It is counter-intuitive behaviour; it goes against our innate sense of self-preservation. Dorothy Rowe, in an article for *Psychologies Magazine*, describes the thankless task of caring for a depressed person as follows:

> *You suggest they see a doctor, and they refuse. You suggest a walk or a meal to cheer them up, and they stay mute or tell you you're an idiot for suggesting something so stupid. If you press them, they turn on you, sometimes nastily, so you can't help feeling hurt. Physically, they retreat from you or worse, push you away. When visitors arrive, the depressed person either races into their room and slams the door, or suddenly becomes his or her usual social self. When the visitors leave, they sink back into silence.*[2]

Who in their right minds would tolerate a situation like this? Why choose to stay?

Why Bother?

For some, it is a calling to be alongside the suffering and they will seek them out, or be sought by them. For many, it is unavoidable, as those we love and live alongside tumble into unannounced mishaps. If we are committed to those in our lives, that commitment calls us to stay put when things get rough.

At my boarding school, homework was done under supervision each evening in a large room with desks around the walls. My desk happened to be between two girls who had taken a particular dislike to me. They had a habit of passing notes across my desk to each other, in such a way as

I was left in no doubt about the subject of the missives (often it was me). One such note said, 'Eugh. She's crying again. Just ignore her – she wants attention.' Later on that same evening, possibly thinking they were being helpful, they gave me this wonderful maxim for life: 'Laugh and the world laughs with you. Cry and you cry alone.' Fortunately that has not been my experience.

We cry with those who cry because that is what love means sometimes. We stay there because we are needed, and we want to do the right thing. We offer comfort because we have been offered comfort, and we know how it felt to have someone there. We walk with people down their lonely pathways because that is what Jesus calls us to do. In his letter to the Romans, Paul spends eleven chapters explaining that salvation is pure gift. There is no way we can earn the right to God's acceptance or approval. Then in chapter twelve he starts to talk about living appropriately in response to receiving a gift such as this. Part of the response involves the way we treat each other, and this is very pertinent to how and why we support those with depression:

> *Be devoted to one another in brotherly love. Honour one another above yourselves... Be joyful in hope, patient in affliction, faithful in prayer. Share with God's people who are in need. Practice hospitality... Rejoice with those who rejoice; mourn with those who mourn. Live in harmony with one another... Do not be conceited.*

Romans 12:10–13, 15–16

Whether you feel equipped and skilled to do this job or not, the job is yours. I hope that I can maybe help you with some ideas and encourage you to keep going.

Number One

Limitations. I mentioned these earlier, and I was beating myself around the head with mine. I'd like to retract some of that verbal head-beating. Because let's face it, we all have them. We are who we are: human, flawed, selfish, and, well, limited. We can't pour ourselves out indefinitely without recharging. So, before we help anyone else, we must look out for Number One (ourselves, not the other person!). Depression can be contagious and we need to make sure we don't catch it or it will be much harder for us to support another person, if not impossible.

If we happen to live with a depressed person, we need to make sure we get out and about and see lots of other, cheerful people, who don't see life as one, huge tragedy. We should talk about lighthearted matters, make daisy-chains, hit a ball around. And we mustn't feel bad that we're not shrouded in gloom too.

It can be helpful to find someone to debrief with. It is probably a good idea to check this out with the depressed person first, and they will, I'm sure, understand that we need someone to talk to. We should ask them to support us as we support the other person. If we can allow ourselves to let off steam with them without feeling bad for being disloyal, it will be a great help in the long run. If we suppress our honest thoughts they might come out in the form of bitterness and anger towards the depressed person and they are probably not in a fit state to take that on board. We can tell our friend when the person is driving us up the wall; when we feel like we can't take it anymore and want to walk out; when we think we have made things worse not better and we don't know what to do. And then we must go back and face the music.

We must make sure we are spiritually nourished; reading our Bibles, going to church, praying. We need to surround ourselves with Godly influences and ask the Spirit to share the burden, to give us love and the stamina that we need, to show us how to be there for them. We can't do it alone. We can do it with God's help.

We have to remind ourselves constantly that it is not up to us to make them better. They cannot depend on us and us alone. They must find their strength within themselves, and from God, and from a variety of people. It is unhealthy, and dangerous even, to be the only person trying to care for someone with depression. If at all possible, avoid this situation. Beware of having a messiah-complex. News flash: we are none of us the messiah.

Dos and Don'ts

For a person who likes to fix things, depression is maddening. If we are to believe the stereotype this might well apply to all men! Sorry guys: this is not something to fix, so put away your screwdriver with its 250 different heads. It can't be fixed, but there are things that can make it easier to bear, and there are things that make it distinctly worse.

One January evening less than a month after getting married, I came home with a day's worth of uncried tears to dispose of. I had no desire to bring my new husband in on this display so I crept in the door and quietly found my way into the darkened bedroom. Once under the covers I let them all out. I was sobbing so hard that I didn't realise Shawn had come in until I felt his arms around me. He lay down beside me and held me for some time without saying anything. I eventually told him to go away and that I would come out when I was more presentable, but he stubbornly refused to leave. It was very embarrassing to let him see me in that state (three years on and I have no dignity to lose!), but I can't express how much it meant to have him just be there. That's the main thing that helps. You may long to be more proactive, to get your hands stuck into a practical solution, but please hear me on this: we really just need you to BE THERE. No fuss, no frills, no beautifully crafted words of advice. A hug and a willingness to listen go a long, long way. Early on this year, my poor little sister was going through a heartbreak. She was at university and three hours away down the motorway, and one evening she really needed me to be there. I had given up my super-powers for Lent, so unfortunately couldn't fly there in supersonic time. Instead we made use of the free-calls-after-six deal and went to sleep on the phone to each other, not saying anything, just lying (a bit uncomfortably if I'm honest) with the receiver to our ears. She told me afterwards that this was comforting, so I pass it on as a tip if you can't be there in person.

Having said all that about just being there, there are some things that can be done that are invaluable to a depressed person. To someone in depression, the practicalities of life can seem overwhelming. I had a friend at university who once came over to tidy my room for me. This simple act of service made such a huge difference. For starters I no longer had to deal with the musty smell and strange crunchy noises as I walked across the floor. If you are able to find a way to do something of this nature it will mean a lot. It may be a case of helping the person write a to-do list, or going with them to an appointment, or just doing the dishes. Be warned though – catch them at the wrong moment and they might take it as a criticism that they can't manage by themselves. It's a tricky business.

When you are depressed you are bombarded with irrational thoughts much of the time. It can be helpful to have someone as a sounding board, someone who can tell you which of your thoughts are truthful and which are completely off course. I have sometimes completely lost the plot. One day I was looking at some family photos with a friend called Penny, and told her straight faced that my family would have been perfect if I were not in it. She told me pretty firmly that I was being ridiculous, and I didn't dare think that particular thought again. If you can bear to sit and listen to the ramblings of a negative and self-absorbed human, and help them to sort their thoughts out, you will be doing them a great service. However, it should be said that you should have clear boundaries in place, as the need for this kind of listening is endless and could swallow you up if you are not careful.

As with small children, distraction can work a treat with depressed people. There is nothing nicer than being given a short holiday from the same dreary thoughts that circle boringly around your mind. Try taking them to the cinema, or if they won't leave the house, put on a DVD. Try to get them to go for a walk, or tell them a silly story about your day. In suggesting things to do, try not to provide too many options as they will struggle with decision making. And never ask open-ended questions like, 'What do you feel like doing?' or 'What can I do to make you feel better?' They will not be able to answer, and the inability to do so will in itself make them feel worse.

A Friend Indeed

I recently came across the story of the friendship between the eighteenth-century poet John Cowper (pronounced Cooper for those to whom these things matter) and John Newton (pronounced Newton), the author of one of our most treasured hymns, 'Amazing Grace'.[3] Cowper was sent to boarding school at the age of six on the death of his mother, where he was horribly bullied. He had four major episodes of depression, survived many suicide attempts and was committed into an asylum for the insane for a year and a half. He converted to Christianity, largely due to the influence of his doctor, Dr Nathaniel Cotton. John Newton was curate of the church at Olney where Cowper came to live. The two of them struck up a deep and sincere friendship, as well as collaborating on a book of hymns. When Newton moved to Lombard Street in London they stayed closely in touch.

Newton was the kind of friend that every person with depression should have. He visited often. On one occasion he gave up his vacation to be with Cowper when he was feeling suicidal. His affection was unwavering, and his patience outstanding. After a visit in 1788, Cowper wrote, 'I found those comforts in our visit, which have formerly sweetened all our interviews, in part restored. I knew you; knew you for the same shepherd who was sent to lead me out of the wilderness into the pasture where the Chief Shepherd feeds his flock, and felt my sentiments of affectionate friendship for you the same as ever.'[4]

He was the kind of friend whose company made one feel better. He also, on occasion, spoke strongly and firmly, which we all need sometimes. His tone was never judgmental, but always full of conviction and strength:

> *Doubt your despairing thoughts. Who do you think you are to make final declarations about your soul that lie hidden in the secrets of the Almighty? No. No. Renounce such confidence. If you have no ability for faith in the love of God for you, make no more such great pretences to have such certainty of faith in your damnation. This is not yours to know. Rather, yours is to listen to Jesus.*[5]

If you have a friend such as that in your life, thank God for them. If you are a friend like that, you are a greater blessing than you will probably ever know: thank you on behalf of depressed people everywhere. I am humbled by and deeply grateful for the number of people who have sacrificially poured themselves out to keep me going during hard times, who really were Christ in the flesh in the love they showed me. It is hard to love someone with depression. Depression does not make people very loveable, and they do not hold up their end of the relationship very well. But when you love someone with depression you are doing what Jesus has called you to do, and he will help you.

Job's Comforters (Or What Not To Say)

I had a lovely card from my friend Janice the other day that concluded, *'p.s. Am reading Job at the moment – how great that God chose to devote a whole book to "How not to treat people who are depressed"!'*

So I reread Job, and she's absolutely right. It's a brilliant example of what to avoid doing and saying when trying to help a depressed person. Job is this fellow who's doing really well in life, until everything goes horribly wrong – his children die (all fourteen of them), his oxen and donkeys are nicked by the Sabeans, his sheep and servants are burned to a crisp, his house is blown down and to cap it all, his skin breaks out in painful sores. He's not a happy chappy.

His friends hear about his troubles and come to 'sympathise with him and comfort him' (2:11) which they do pretty well to begin with:

> *When they saw him from a distance, they could hardly recognise him; they began to weep aloud, and they tore their robes and sprinkled dust on their heads. Then they sat on the ground with him for seven days and seven nights. No one said a word to him, because they saw how great his suffering was.*

Job 2:12–13

But before long, they blow it completely. We know from chapter one that Job is a righteous and good man, with high standing in God's eyes. Job's friends, however, assume that he must have somehow called down his troubles on his own head, and all three attempt to convince him of this, as though admitting his guilt will make his circumstances improve.

Eliphaz, having buttoned his lip for a week, can't hold it in any longer ('If someone ventures a word with you, will you be impatient? But who can keep from speaking?' 4:2). His contribution can basically be summarised as follows: 'You've been strong in the past, mate. Think about those times and don't let this get you down. No one good ever gets knocked down for long. Pray to God and he'll do a miracle and make it all better. And you're lucky mate: God's giving you a work out for your long-term benefit. You see, your life will be brilliant in no time flat!' He is applying simple rules that don't work, and putting much of the onus of the situation on Job. If you try to follow that strategy it will only serve to enrage or discourage. Life just doesn't work like that. Job responds in this vein, 'I don't think you realise quite how dreadful I feel, Eliphaz, you irritating little man. You insult me with your cheery clichés. You just can't cope with seeing me this way and you're trying to whitewash things. You are utterly useless as a friend' (chapter 6). Warning: depressed people can be HARSH if you say the wrong thing!

Zophar also tries to square things up rationally. He figures that Job must have done something to cause his misfortunes, thus, to put it right he need only repent: 'If you put away the sin that is in your hand and allow no evil to dwell in your tent, then, free of fault you will lift up your face. You will stand firm and without fear.' (11:14–15). Job does not take kindly to this diagnosis. For starters, Zophar is speaking for God, and putting himself in a superior position. It is all very well to make judgments like this when things are going well for you. How would it feel if the tables were turned? Try to avoid looking for faults that could have led to depression. It will make the person feel worse, and they will already be more than aware of their shortcomings.

Bildad, like an elephant trying to make doll's furniture, delivers his helpful summary of the situation: 'Awful things happen to evil people. Therefore, you are evil.' Great. Thanks friend. Job replies, 'How long will you torment me and crush me with words? Just SHUT UP and stop judging me!' roughly paraphrased.

In summary, Job's assessment of their counselling skills is

as follows:

My brothers are as undependable as intermittent streams. (6:15)
You have proved to be of no help. (6:21)
You are worthless physicians, all of you!
If only you would be altogether silent! (13:4–5)
You are miserable comforters, all of you!
Will your long-winded speeches never end?
What ails you that you keep on arguing? (16:2–3)

Ouch! It is surely a thankless task trying to help such a person. I think from this short foray into the book of Job, we can see the main thing required in this situation. I will let our main protagonist spell it out:

Listen carefully to my words;
Let this be the consolation you give me.
Bear with me while I speak.

Job 21:2–3

Forgiveness

Are you familiar with the parable of the ungrateful servant in Matthew 18? It goes something like this: a man has a servant, Bob, who owes him, on a conservative estimate, about three trillion pounds. He, rather generously, decides to cancel the debt, which was never going to get paid anyway as it would take several hundred years on Bob's current salary. So Bob is very pleased about this and goes down to the pub to celebrate. He's leaning on the bar with his pint, bragging about it to his mates, when in walks Bert, who owes him a tenner. He thumps his drink down, sloshing a bit onto the floor, gets poor Bert by the collar and demands his money back. Bert is unemployed and only has a couple of quid in his pocket, so Bob calls the coppers and Bert is thrown into the slammer until he can repay.

So there is the rationale for forgiveness – God forgave us

so we would be horribly mean-spirited not to forgive others. I mention forgiveness in this context because in going through depression we will inevitably have been let down, hurt, neglected, ignored, abandoned, mocked, undermined, and misunderstood. And we must forgive the perpetrators of these crimes. Likewise, in caring for those who are depressed, you will have been insulted, snubbed, blamed, avoided, bruised (definitely emotionally, maybe physically too), and cried on till your clothes were ruined by their salty tears. You too must forgive. These are genuine wrongs. They are not acceptable. But they must be forgiven.

Chapter 6

Relationships

The basis for any relationship with another person is our relationship with ourselves. Depression makes this relationship tricky, as it throws our whole identity into confusion. Much of what we have learnt to be true about who we are changes. We are not sure how to relate to ourselves let alone others.

For the years when depression was a significant part of my life, I felt like I was two people. The one I liked better, Happy-Jo, would make friends, make people laugh, have a lot to give. The problem was, at any moment Depressed-Jo could make an appearance and undo all the good work. Depressed-Jo was whiney, quiet, paranoid, needy, under-confident. Imagine that Happy-Jo applied for a job and was given an interview. What would happen if Depressed-Jo was the one to turn up on the all-important day? Disaster:

Interviewer: So, Depressed-Jo, tell us a little about yourself.

D-J: I am as you can see, very ugly. I have failed at everything I've tried to do, which isn't much because I usually waste opportunities that come my way, and I can tell you confidently that everyone who meets me dislikes me. My hobbies include lying under my duvet and eating junk food until I feel sick.

Interviewer: Ah. Well, perhaps you could give us an idea of what you would bring to our organisation?

D-J: I would bring an atmosphere of sadness and gloom. I would have low expectations of myself and others that I can guarantee would be met. I would ensure you re-ordered tissues whenever stocks ran low.

Interviewer: Why should we hire you for this position Depressed-Jo?

D-J: I really wouldn't. I have nothing to give and I am likely to be a burden on your resources. I don't even know why I came today. I am so sorry for wasting your time. It must have been my associate, Happy-Jo, who filled out the job application – she usually over-estimates my abilities.

While it is confusing for the depressed person to be so different when depressed, it is equally so for friends and family who witness this transformation. Mental illness is a fearsome thing in that it affects the core of an identity; the very seat of character and personality is thrown into disarray, leaving the onlookers bewildered and afraid. I have seen this happen suddenly with a woman who suffered an extreme form of psychosis: in the middle of a conversation about her upcoming marriage, she leapt to her feet, brandished a chair in the air and began to address voices only she could hear. My depression has been more insidious, creeping over the horizon like a Welsh fog, but changing the essential me nonetheless. How do you cope when someone you know seems to be a different person? What happens to the relationship?

It is tempting to withdraw from relationships of all kinds when depressed. We must fight this instinct. Don Miller tells of how he had become increasingly isolated at one stage in his life and how his pastor urged him to live in a house with other guys from the church to counteract this trend:

> *Rick told me, a little later, I should be living in community. He said I should have people around bugging me and getting under my skin because without people I could not grow – I could not grow in God, and I could not grow as a human. We are born into*

*families, he said, and we are needy at first as children because _
God wants us together, living among one another, not hiding
ourselves under logs like fungus. 'You are not a fungus,' he told
me, 'you are a human, and you need other people in your life in
order to be healthy.'[1]*

Relationships with Family

These days families are much less of a solid proposition. I
know that a significant proportion of you who are reading
this will have divorced parents. Most of you will live
hundreds of miles away from anyone you're related to. You
will have halves and steps and all manner of permutations to
the traditional unit. You will have estranged cousins in
Australia (why do they always live in Australia?) and
grandparents who cut you out of the will. You might have
had the sperm part of you bought on eBay, or have been a
foetus inside your aunt. Whatever your situation, there will
still be people in this world who belong to you in a way that
is unique: other relationships you choose; families you are
given.

I happen to come from a traditional setup. In my 'family
of origin' there are parents who have been married for nearly
thirty years to date, and three girls and one boy. We have one
grandmother left, but grew up with strong, involved
relationships with all four grandparents. We have four sets of
aunts and uncles and an average number of cousins. There
are no feuds, no secrets (or none that have been let out of the
bag yet anyway!). My immediate family, the six Harrises, as
we then were, has become subdivided as three of us have got
married. Esther has found Rob, and they live in South Africa
at the moment. Jem joined forces with Davy and they live in
Vancouver. Shawn and I are here in Chalfont St Peter and
Mum and Dad are based in France. Bethie is in Birmingham
learning to be a nurse. Even with all this distance and the

additions to the group, we are still a strong unit and our commitment to each other is concrete: whatever happens, there will always be a relationship between all of us that can't be called into question.

Perhaps, then, there is licence for greater carelessness. My family have been the brunt of quite self-indulgent behaviour on my part, because I had the safety to let it all hang out. I could show up at mealtimes and sit there silently like a rain cloud. I could yell, 'You have no idea what I'm going through' and slam doors. I could dump blame and condemnation on their heads: 'You made me wear horrible second-hand clothes and let me get bad haircuts so it's your fault I got bullied at school.' I could, in short, get away with being a wretch, and abuse the strength of blood ties. Over time we have been able to talk and forgive and even laugh about some of these episodes, but I do wish I had been more careful of the people I love the most in the world.

While family relationships are the backdrop of our lives it is easy to take them for granted. But they do suffer if not cared for and treated well. If you have a family who love you, that is a precious, precious thing. Be careful of how your depression causes you to treat it.

Your family probably knows you better than anyone and it will be hardest of all for them to understand the transformation that depression brings about. If they seem baffled and unsure of how to relate to you, give them some slack. Try to explain how you feel without lashing out angrily because they don't intuitively understand.

Relationships with Friends

When I was at my school in Portugal, the scarcity of friends was a pressing concern. Due to the transience of the ex-pat community in the Algarve, there were always new people arriving and before each term started Mum and I would pray that there would be a friend for me in the new crop of pupils.

I would buzz hopefully up to the new person and try to suss out if they were my answer to prayer. The problem was that my efforts were always swiftly sabotaged by my classmates who would inform the object of my advances that to be friends with me would be social suicide. If the new person was not worth rescuing from this fate then they would be left to me, and we would form an uneasy alliance of the outcast, walking around the edge of the playground together trying to find more common ground than our mutual exclusion. I had one 'friend', Georgina, who would eat half of my packed lunch every day in addition to her own. I allowed this plundering to go on, knowing that if I put a step wrong I could be entirely alone in the jungle. As it happened she was judged more acceptable than me by the tribe and I was unceremoniously dumped one lunch break (after she'd eaten half my mini Mars Bar). Even though I didn't really like her, and could now have my whole lunch to myself each day, it was a traumatic loss.

Later I discovered the joy of genuine friendship, friendship forged from mutual liking and respect, shared experience and humour, common goals. Maybe because of those early experiences of loneliness, friends are insanely important to me. I love my friends so, so much. You would too if you met them. They are funny, honest, interesting and kind. I have moved around a lot so they live all over the place, and our contact can be sporadic – I look forward to heaven when I can hopefully get my favourite people all together. Bliss. Sometimes, like now, when I am writing and doing a full-time job, I am not very good at staying in touch. But I think about them and pray for them and know they won't give up on me.

When I get low, I panic that I will lose all my friends. I won't be able to sustain the relationships and it will be too much for them to hold it together by themselves. They will get fed up of waiting for me to perk up. They'll forget what I was like when I wasn't depressed and why they became friends with me in the first place. I am liable to snap at them and be hurtful. I will stand them up for arrangements that I can't keep because I'm not up to leaving the house.

People are people not angels, so I can't say that my fears have been entirely unfounded. This is partly because I send out messages that I don't want their friendship and make myself scarce. I have to take responsibility for that. But I do have a number who have stayed true blue throughout. Over time I have realised who these people are, and learned to invest in these relationships and not overextend to those who will fall away as soon as trouble arrives. We can't have infinite numbers of deep relationships in our lives. It is far better, I think, to limit who we really welcome into the inner circle.

Friends are precious gifts from God and life without them would be dull indeed. I am so grateful for the people who have graced my life like jewels (I am starting to sound a bit like Anne of Green Gables here!). I do mean it though.

Relationship with Spouse

I met Shawn on September 12th 2001. I remember this date because it was the day after the terrorist attacks in the US, and that whole autumn I felt out of kilter with the solemnity of the times – I was truly happy.

Three weeks after we first met, Shawn asked me out for coffee one day while I was working at the bookstore. We went that evening and when Starbucks kicked us out at closing time, we walked down to the beach at Spanish Banks and mooched along the shoreline finding we really liked each other's company. As we said goodbyes on the porch of my house at 2 a.m., there was a sense that this was going to be something important.

Vancouver is a delightfully romantic city in which to kick off a relationship. We went to the snowy top of Grouse Mountain on a ski lift to look at the lights, we had weekends on secluded gulf islands, we snuggled on sofas in cosy coffee-shops and walked around Stanley Park in the rain. It was the easiest, most obvious thing in the world to be together. It made sense, and it made us happy.

I started going for counselling around then, which was strange in a way because I had never felt so far from needing it, but I knew the depression was going to keep cropping up unless I did something about it. I felt a bit embarrassed telling Shawn and worried it would make him think I was going to be too high-maintenance to bother with, but he was supportive and not at all fazed.

While we were dating, and engaged, I just about stayed out of a proper depression. I teetered on the edge once or twice, but never fell in. Every now and then I tried to explain to Shawn that he might have to deal with another side to me at some point and that it would be hard for him, but it was in the abstract and didn't worry him. Shawn is a very sunny person on the whole, very even tempered. He had quite a rough up-bringing so this is a surprising quality. He should be the one with the emotional issues not me. Anyway, on our honeymoon, I started crying and didn't stop for about four months. By then he had promised to take me, better or worse, sickness or health, till death did us part. HA! He couldn't escape! I felt like I'd tricked him into marrying me while I was OK and then pulled a whole new proposition out of the bag once the deal was signed and sealed. I really did feel sorry for him. Maybe this is what every marriage involves in a sense. Mike Mason, in his beautiful meditation, *The Mystery of Marriage*, writes this:

> *marriage is a relationship far more engrossing than we want it to be. It always turns out to be more than we bargained for. It is disturbingly intense, disruptively involving, and that is exactly the way it was designed to be. It is supposed to be more, almost, than we can handle. It was meant to be a lifelong encounter that*

would be much more rigorous and demanding than anything human beings ever could have chosen, dreamed of, desired, or invented on their own.[2]

Shawn and I were thrown into the truth of this from day one. The strength of our vows was immediately put to the test: I'd be lying if I told you that depression didn't put strain on a marriage. There was NEVER any question whether Shawn would stick it out or not: his love and commitment didn't waver for a second, but he did tell me I needed a kick in the butt once and he didn't want me to go on antidepressants. I battled the instinct to retreat on a daily basis, tempted to hide the reality of what I was feeling at the expense of an honest relationship. I was so afraid I'd lose his love and respect. It still amazes me that I didn't: God has blessed me with a wonderful husband.

Marriage is painful grace. We do not earn or deserve the love of the other – it is there as a gift, and we must accept it or risk eroding the foundations of the fort that is there to protect us. Once the vows are said, something mystical takes place, and God makes us one. The sorrows of one become the sorrows of the other. We are one flesh. In the midst of my misery during those months my eyes were opened to the enormity of the commitment we had walked into, and it was overwhelming. I was never going to be alone in my depression in the way I had been before.

Each marriage is its own country, and no foreigner can understand its language or customs. I am loath to make any pronouncements more generalised than about my own marriage. Depression will make its inroads, but they will look different in every marriage. For ours I can say that it magnified the fact of our commitment being bigger than ourselves, and God's ability to give us the resources to live that out. It has stretched our resolve to love one another selflessly, to die to self, and in that it was strangely good. Had it gone on longer than a few months I might be saying different things altogether – I don't know.

Companionship

We need people around us at the best of times, more so at the worst. Depression builds a wall around us that threatens to cut us off from the rest of the human race and it takes work on our part and on the part of those who care for us to attack that wall with sledgehammers and make sure we don't get locked away for good.

Depression does impact our relationships – of course it does. It impacts our ability to love and receive love because it undermines our sense of self and distorts our perspective. We believe wholeheartedly in the lie that we are horrible scum and don't want to inflict ourselves on others. We need to face the fact that our depression is going to be a challenge to those around us. But at the same time, we must not at any cost, remove ourselves because we need those relationships to stay alive. And there will be those whose love is strong enough to carry us, and who are committed to us whatever the circumstances.

Chapter 7

Suicide

It is common for those who are depressed to dwell on death. It usually comes with the territory. Life is painful and hard and because of your illness, you are unable to conceive of a future that is any better. Death seems to offer the only hope of relief. For the vast majority, these thoughts remain thoughts, and no effort is made to actively seek out death. However, there are those who take the decision to end their own lives, in a devastatingly final attempt to end their suffering and escape from a seemingly untenable reality. Of those, many do not succeed. Some, tragically, do.

When depressed, I used to have grizzly fantasies of car accidents and cancer, the angel of death swooping in to rescue me from having to endure another minute of my existence. On only two occasions did I seriously consider taking action. The first was a cold February day in Birmingham. I was walking along the Bristol Road, heading into campus for a lecture. The traffic was heavy and fast moving and it occurred to me that a small step would take me into the path of a car that could probably kill me. I realised with a shock that I really wanted to take that step, and grabbed hold of the grimy railings to hold myself back.

The second was while I was working part-time as a receptionist just after graduating from my Masters. I was finding it quite stressful, and was clashing with the other receptionist. That particular day, she had told me that she'd had a meeting with our boss and they'd decided that if I didn't get better at the job in two weeks I'd be fired. This blew me apart to a disproportionate degree. I rushed home and worked myself up into a completely hysterical state, culminating in a search through the bathroom cabinets for all the medication I could find. Then I calmed down enough to realise I really didn't want to do anything that drastic, and called my friend Catherine who stayed on the phone saying just the right things until Shawn got home.

Survivors

I came to know Suzannah when she stayed at the epilepsy centre for a couple of months in 2005. I was her keyworker, and whilst I had a professional duty of care towards her, I also rapidly discovered an enormous amount of large and small things that we had in common: we were the same height and weight, we were both left-handed, we had passed our driving tests on the second attempt, we had the same Myers-Briggs personality types, we were both Christians, both slightly rebellious and outspoken, and we had both experienced depression. Before I met her, I had read through her medical notes and knew she was coming to us one week after being discharged from a psychiatric hospital, where she was staying following her third suicide attempt. This fact registered with me but didn't hit home with any force until I had become extremely fond of her bubbly laugh, good natured teasing, willingness to enter into honest and deep conversation. Looking at her wide, smiling eyes, chaotic curly hair and cheeky grin I found it almost impossible to reconcile the person before me with the Suzannah who had emptied a box of carefully hoarded clobazam into her despairing body and gone to sleep hoping never to wake up.

We sat in a quiet corner one day and she told me unflinchingly, 'I meant it, Jo. I meant to die, and I was really angry when it didn't work.' She told me of the spiral of anguish that had led to that night: 'I loved my job as a neo-natal nurse, and when I started having seizures and was told I couldn't carry on it was devastating. I felt like my purpose in life had been taken away. Eventually I got another job, doing medical research but the people I worked with told me they didn't think I was up to it and my boss tried to get me fired. I struggled to contest it, getting the unions involved and it even went to tribunal, but eventually I just gave up. Then one weekend I had a good friend to stay. We had such a great time together, but still underneath I felt just awful. The day she left I got into bed and didn't get up for over twenty-four hours and I was thinking, "Is this how my life is going to be now?" I couldn't stand it. I went to do some weeding in the graveyard at our church and my little dog was running around happily, and I thought how he would be taken care of by my parents, and how my parents had each other and my sister had her husband, and that was it. I decided I had to get out. I went home and took the pills, and waited for it all to end.' As it turned out, a friend came round and found her in time.

Hazrabi is from Southall. She is too heavy for conventional weighing scales: she can't sit in chairs with arms and can only walk short distances. Last May she attended a relative's wedding celebrations in India. With the other female attendants, she underwent numerous beauty treatments and swathed herself in a fine, if voluminous, new sari. Feeling more attractive than usual, she was devastated to catch a glimpse of herself in a mirror, seeing 'a great big heifer' staring back at her. She fell into a deep depression and sometime later took an overdose, convinced her fat made her worthless and deserving of nothing but death.

Eve was one of my housemates in Canada. She was an amazingly gifted and creative person, spending her days on little projects such as delicately balanced mobiles made of the beautiful fall leaves, and homemade paper. She was quiet and gentle and had selflessly befriended an impoverished Russian immigrant family in our neighbourhood, whom she unobtrusively cared for in numerous practical ways. Every now and then she would go missing for a few days, and my other housemates told me this was not unusual for her and there was no need to worry. When the days turned into over a week one autumn, we did begin to worry, and we eventually tracked her down in the psychiatric wing of the university hospital. She had tried to kill herself and been found wandering, confused and very sick, through the endowment lands.[1]

And Others

Louise was someone I knew at university. She was a lesbian and felt that all Christians were against her because of her sexuality, so it was hard to form any sort of friendship, although we did have some good conversations and often ended up at the same strange African cultural events around Birmingham. On the first morning of our finals I had a phone call – 'Louise has killed herself.' The exams we had revised for so unstintingly over the previous weeks became at once insignificant as our small department converged in grief and disbelief under the old Joe clock tower on campus. It emerged that she had gone missing the night before, and sometime after, had made her way to the main railway station and jumped from a bridge in front of an approaching train. We spent the next week meeting as a group, talking about her, crying, trying to accustom ourselves to her absence.

When I was fifteen, a girl in my year at school was missing from class for a couple of weeks. She came back strangely silent, with dark circles under her eyes. On a cross country 'run' (we were in the unkindly named 'The Dropouts' and were not really expected to go faster than an amble, a suitable speed for conducting long conversations) she told me her father had driven to a local beauty spot and shot himself in the head in response to learning of a personal financial crisis. Her life would never be the same again.

My friend Sam went to collect his aunt for a family lunch one Sunday. He was appalled to find her covered in blood, wrists slit, and a glass of brandy unfinished at her side. The image will never fade for him. As a newly qualified paramedic he did his best to revive her until the emergency services arrived, but without success. As he recounted the incident to me the trauma was evident in his eyes, despite the intervening years.

Why?

The most obvious motivation for suicide is a desire not to live. There comes a point where anything is preferable to current circumstances. There are however many other reasons why people choose to end their own lives. It could be the avoidance of shame, as in the case of my schoolmate's father, who could not live with the fact of his financial downfall. For some it is to avoid a more painful death. This is seen sometimes in patients with terminal cancer who decide to end things before they become too grim. Suicide can be a form of revenge, a way of punishing those who have hurt you, perhaps a lover who has left or the bullies who torment you at school or at work. Guilt for a suicide is a life-long blight. Suicide can come out of religious conviction in some cases, as it apparently is for the Islamic suicide bombers who die believing their sacrifice has gained them certain welcome into heaven. There have been examples of this amongst extremist cults also, such as the People's Temple in Guyana, which carried out a mass suicide in 1978. Lastly, some suicides are the tragic result of mental illness. An acquaintance of mine told me once that she lived with a constant stream of voices forcibly telling her to end her life, and exactly how to go about it. She felt compelled to obey.

Ground Zero

Suicide cuts down unique individuals but conducts a common inquisition of those who remain.[2]

For some people the temptation to end it can't be resisted, the means are too convenient and the alternative untenable. Solomon argues that the very possibility of suicide makes depression bearable by providing an escape route for the eventuality of reaching the limits of toleration: 'Knowing that if I get through this minute I could always kill myself in the next one makes it possible to get through this minute without being utterly overwhelmed. Suicidality may be a symptom of depression; it is also a mitigating factor.'[3]

What may seem like a tidy solution on the spur of the moment, however, unfailingly leaves a trail of devastation in its wake. To grieve for someone whose death was at their own hands is a messy business. Of course there is the normal sense of loss and sadness, the emptiness of the places they had walked, the debris of their existence left to be redistributed or destroyed – clothing, books, journals, travel mementoes and Christmas gifts. The memories take on the surreal hue of fantasy, and we work to catalogue and preserve a collection that will not now be added to: a complete oeuvre locked in time. But then there is an additional parade of ugly emotions. We feel anger: they put us through this turmoil. They chose to give us this weighty burden. We feel rejection. They did not love us enough to stay. We feel shame. We did not see it coming, we could not prevent it, we are perhaps to blame...

Some try desperately to find hope and even heroism in the act. My English seminar group decided that the ending of Kate Chopin's *The Awakening* was the culmination of a triumphant release from fettering ties and obligations as the main subject of the novel walked into the sea until the waters closed over her head and she drowned. 'No! NO NO NO!' I wanted to scream. There is nothing redemptive or good in suicide and let no one say otherwise.[4]

A bereavement of any kind is isolating, as friends and acquaintances draw away in awkwardness or fear, unsure of how to offer solace. In the case of a suicide the isolation can be so much worse. There is still a taboo that throws a long shadow of secrecy over the subject. People speculate in private about the details, and probe the motivations, but the horror of it makes it hard to bring it into the open. The people who are grieving over suicides need our support and love and presence as much or more so than those who have died of natural causes or accidents. We need to walk over the thin ice of scandal and sensationalism and put our arms around the hurting person who needs us.

Prevention

Sometimes it is possible to tell if someone (including yourself) is at serious risk of ending their own life. Generally it is when there is a plan in place and the means to carry it out. This is not foolproof, needless to say, so please don't feel over-responsible – some people will vocalise these things for drama and attention, and others who really do want to carry it through will keep it carefully private. If you do feel there is a serious risk present there are things you can do. First, make sure the person is not alone for any length of time. This might necessitate a hospital admission or sectioning if the person is not amenable. The Samaritans are always on the end of a phone line and are wonderfully competent to deal with this sort of situation. Second, make sure that you get rid of the means: knives, pills, rope, whatever could be used in this way. Third, tell people about the situation. This is a hard thing to do, but if it is you who wants to commit suicide you need an army of people to protect you, and if you are someone who is supporting that person, you cannot do it unaided.

Suicide and Christians

There is a deep silence around the topic of suicide: it is rarely written about, less often spoken of. Official statistics are universally acknowledged to be inaccurate, due to 'religious and bureaucratic prejudices, family sensitivity, the vagaries and differences in the proceedings of coroners' courts and post-mortem examinations, the shadowy distinctions between suicides and accidents – in short, personal, official and traditional unwillingness to recognise the act for what it is'.[5] If this is true in wider society it is even more so the case in the church, where great theological confusion is added to the mix.

In the Bible there are a few examples of suicide, but each is presented without comment: Saul and his armour bearer fall on their own swords (1 Samuel 31:4–5), Ahithrophel hanged himself (2 Samuel 17:23), Zimri set his palace on fire and died in the flames (1 Kings 16:18), and Judas Iscariot hanged himself (Matthew 27:5).

In times gone by, the church has made its pronouncement by forbidding the burial of suicides inside the church yard, the inference being that they have fallen outside the grace of God. Augustine, immeasurably influential in the formation of early Christian thought, argued in his work, 'City of God' that suicide is a form of homicide and repentance of such an act was unlikely. Considered Christian opinion still holds that suicide is morally wrong,[6] but our God is merciful and gracious and does not judge us as we deserve, but rather has accepted the perfect righteousness of Jesus, his beloved son, as sufficient for our salvation. John White writes:

> Let us grant that suicide is not only tragic but sinful. Let us accept that life is a precious gift from God and that issues of life and death belong to their Author. But let us look on those who take their lives with the compassion with which Jesus looked on all sinners. Indeed, if compassion is called for, surely some suicide victims call for more compassion than other sinners.[7]

There are no easy answers to be had for the eternal resting place of those who have taken their own life. God alone knows, and all we can do is bow to his sovereignty and trust in his perfect goodness, love and compassion.

Chapter 8

Survival

Depression makes life difficult and it can be tempting to feel extremely sorry for yourself. I have held many a pity-party for myself for this very reason. Other people can wake up, spring out of bed and go about their daily business without a care in the world: why should I have to deal with wanting to die with the rising of the sun each day? While I am as opposed to the 'pull yourself together' type of sympathy as anyone, I do believe we have a choice about how we live with our depression. We can either lie down and give in to it (I have tried this and it gets boring after about ten minutes: you'd think something dramatic would happen to mark such a drastic decision, like the earth breaking open to receive your living corpse – it doesn't). Or we can fight, exhausting and unfair as it may be that we should have to. We can choose, day after yucky day, to pick ourselves up, arm ourselves with courage and survive.

If you are reading this and are going through a time of depression I would like to share some of the strategies I developed over the years in my own bid for survival. I am not by any means an expert in the sense of having studied or trained to come up with these. They come out of the crucible of my experience and I offer them to you as someone who has struggled as you maybe struggle. I found them sometimes helpful, and therefore maybe you will. Some types of depression are so debilitating that even the thought of reading a plan let alone starting on point one can be enough activity for the day. If that is you, maybe you should skip this chapter or save it till you are stronger. Otherwise, add the ones that appeal to your arsenal, and fight the good fight.

Handy Hints and Clever Tips

Read and Memorise Truthful Things

I have found it helpful to have truthful things in writing that I can read and use in place of thoughts when my thoughts are dragging me down. I had chunks of the Bible memorised and sometimes simple phrases such as 'the joy of the Lord is my strength' would keep me going. I also had a couple of letters from my mum, and cards from friends, with lovely, affirming, truthful things in them that I had handy at all times.

Prepare for Your Black Spots

Identifying the worst times of day and then coming up with a plan to deal with them was always very important for me. Waking up was usually a bad time. At university my lovely housemate Bekah would come down to my room and bring me tea, and sometimes sit with me while I drank it so that I wouldn't be alone. Shawn would also make me tea and then we would read the Bible and pray together. If you live by yourself, you could ask a friend to give you a quick phone call first thing. It might be the early afternoon that gets to you: in that case, maybe arrange to meet a friend for a walk or leave the most enjoyable thing on your to-do list for that slot. Anticipation and preparation can make all the difference.

Write Lists

I have found that when I am depressed I am usually very anxious too, and find small tasks overwhelming. Soon everything can seem out of control. One way I have combated this is by making lists, including even the smallest tasks such as brushing my teeth. That way I can approach things bit by bit, and feel a sense of achievement when I complete something. It also reminds me that there are a finite number of jobs to get done – it can be easy to think that it is all impossible and I will never keep the balls in the air. If you can look at a list it controls the panic (cunning idea: put a few things on the list you have already done and put big ticks by them). I have occasionally asked someone to help me put the list together as my mind is too scattered to think clearly.

Get Some Exercise

It is well known that exercise is beneficial to emotional health. During one of my worst periods of depression, my sister Esther made me start running with her. We were in France for the summer, and she had been a trooper – patiently and loyally keeping me company as I bobbed around on the muddy ocean bed. The exercise idea was probably a last resort: it was hot and humid, and I am as sporty as an elderly slug. We started by jogging a few paces then walking a long way then jogging a few paces, by which point I would fall over from exhaustion. I would then crawl home to lie in a dark room and try to recover my ability to breath, and she would do a sneaky marathon without so much as breaking a sweat. Unbelievable. But I did improve bit by bit, and came to enjoy my daily totter around the village, Estie's encouragement ringing in my ears every step ('Keep going Jo! You can do it! Yesterday you had to stop here: now look at you – still running!').

Even if all you can manage is a stagger around the block I would make it a real priority to get moving. Your body will produce endorphins, it will take you out of your usual environment and it might distract your mind for a short time.

Treat Yourself

I found it helpful to identify small treats and to use them as a reward for achieving a certain goal. These have included cups of tea, taking baths, reading a good novel, phoning someone I like for a chat, watching a film... If you plan some of these into your day it can give you something to look forward to, which amounts to hope, which is a good thing! My best treat at the moment is hot chocolate with Baileys: in fact I have just had one now. Mmmm.

Laugh

There is a saying that laughter is the best medicine. There are some who have taken this saying to extremes, for example Dr Madan Kataria, who founded a laughter club in 1995 in Bombay where members were encouraged to laugh loud and long for no reason. It proved so successful that it has spread to many other parts of the world. The physical and psychological benefits of laughter are scientifically documented and whether it takes spending time with a funny friend, watching a silly comedy or simply following the advice of Dr Kataria and laughing as an exercise I would heartily recommend it. Here are some of my best jokes to get you going:

Q. What is green, has four legs, and would kill you if it fell from a tree onto your head?
A. A snooker table
Q. What is brown and sticky?
A. A stick.
Q. What do you call a fly with no wings?
A. A walk.

Sorry: bit lame! They make me laugh anyway.

Do Something for Someone Else

In February 2005 *Time Magazine* did a special issue on the science of Happiness.[1] Among other steps towards leading a more satisfying life it included the advice to do something for someone else. The rationale given was that it will make you feel good about yourself and induce reciprocated kindness. I would want to add that, in the context of depression, it can counter the self-absorption (essentially selfishness) that the condition can involve: it can remind you that there are other beings on the planet and that you can be of service. In *The Back of the North Wind* George Macdonald comments sagely that, '...to try to make others comfortable is the only way to get right comfortable ourselves, and that comes partly of not being able to think so much of ourselves when we are helping other people. For our Selves will always do pretty well if we don't pay them too much attention. Our Selves are like some little children who will be happy enough so long as they are left to their own games, but when we interfere with them, and make them presents of too many sweet things, they begin at once to fret and spoil.'[2]

The time I have most been made aware of the truth of this principle was while I was spending a summer at L'Arche in the North of France. L'Arche, for those of you not familiar with it, is an organisation consisting of small communities of people with physical and mental handicaps and those with more hidden brokenness (the assistants, such as myself). During my time there I was emotionally a big mess. One day I had woken up feeling particularly sorry for myself, and while giving one of my charges a shower began crying rather hopelessly. As I continued to soap her and scrub her down I experienced a change of heart. I was forced out of my own situation in my need to care for her in her funny shaped body and muddled mind. It was in a small way a very profound experience and one I have often looked back on as I have tried to reach out of myself in times of depression.

Make Friends with an Animal

Animals are wonderful companions for those with depression. My little cat Ella is snuggled on my lap as I write. She likes to be as close as is felinely possible and with her in the house I never feel alone. Once when I was having a hard day I had run myself a bath and was sitting in the steam preoccupied with my troubles, when her head peeped over the edge with such a look of astonishment that I laughed out loud. She proceeded to prance up and down the precariously slippery side fishing for my toes and being taken by surprise by the water each time her paw touched the surface. I have a friend who has a terrier to whom she attributes her emotional survival, as she is forced to care for another life: taking him for walks gets her out of the house, feeding him gets her out of bed in the morning, playing with him takes her out of her head. If you don't have a pet, see if someone will let you play with theirs.

Be Creative

There is a well known link between creativity and depression: some of the best music, paintings and literature come from the depths of human experience: you might produce something really good! Creativity is enormously life giving and grounding. You do not need to be traditionally 'artistic' to be creative – your outlet could be gardening, carpentry, cooking, making clothes, throwing around clay on a wheel, dancing wildly around your bedroom to eighties pop, or sedately around a community centre gym to a waltz...

Say 'Thank You' Prayers

Keep these short and punchy and refuse to listen to the unhelpful voice that says 'You have nothing to be grateful for' or 'Look how much you have to be grateful for and you're still snivelling you pathetic wretch!' Search for good until you find it, in the smile of a stranger, the colour of a leaf in the gutter, the smell of clean laundry. Thank God for these as they come up and make it a habit to do so. It will eventually train your mind to look up not down.

Pay Attention to Your Dreams

Dreams can be very useful tools for unlocking the secrets of how we feel about things, and can provide clues about how to proceed. Sometimes depression can be the result of repressed emotion, or deep confusion about a situation in our lives, and reading our dreams could throw significant light on things. There are many theories of dream interpretation out there. What I tend to do is pay attention to the feelings in the dream rather than the particular details, and very often the feelings do relate to something going on in my life. I'll tell you about two particularly significant dreams I have had.

The first was during a time I was trying to decide whether I should marry an ex-boyfriend. He had given me a month to think about it, and I was going up the wall thinking of pros and cons and whys and why nots until I really had no idea what I thought or felt in the middle of it all. All I knew was that the outcome of my decision would affect the rest of my life, and the enormity of it paralysed me. So then I had the dream. I was getting married in a huge, dark cathedral, and I was wearing a black wedding dress. All the guests were weeping, and there was a sense of looming disaster about the whole occasion. When I woke up, I realised with a jolt that I really, really did not want to marry this chap.

The second was while I was studying in Vancouver. I had been there about a year, and the dream was as follows. I left a house to go for a walk, but found I couldn't get back – roads and fences kept changing and twisting in the maddening fashion of dreamscapes, and by the time I did return, some inordinate amount of time had passed. The house was quiet and appeared abandoned, but I eventually came across my youngest sister, Bethan, in one of the rooms. She was crying and not realising who I was, told me that it was her fault I had left. The dream stayed with me all day, and it left me with an overpowering sadness that I had moved away with no thought for what it would do to my relationship with my sister. I had gone to boarding school when she was six, and I really felt there was a danger that we could lose any sense of connection. I felt awful that I had not paid the slightest attention to this situation. By the end of the day I had decided to go back to Europe that summer to spend time with her, and I am sure that is the main reason we are so close these days – she is one of my very best friends in the world.

Find Safe Places

My safe places are my bed, anywhere where my husband is holding me tight, and my parents' house in France (if they are at home). These are places I know I am contained and protected and have temporary relief from struggling to be OK and pretend I am fine. I know I can't stay there indefinitely, but going there gives me strength.

Find Safe People

We all have our gifts and some people are gifted with the ability to support and care for the suffering. Find these people and stick close – they are lifesavers! What's more, it will give them joy to help you, because this is how they are wired, and God made them for this purpose. It is usually good to have several of these people up your sleeve though, because you want to share out the responsibility and it's never good to become too dependent on any one human (become as dependent as you like on God though).

Avoid Unsafe People

I am sure you have come across people who unfailingly make you feel worse. They will say, with ill-concealed irritation and impatience, 'Just look at everything you have going for you. Cheer up for goodness sake!' Or they will sit there uncomfortably while you cry until the first opportunity they can reasonably bolt. Or they will ask helplessly, 'What is it *now*?' and if they can't fix you in thirty seconds they will get cross. Identify the people who make you feel worm-like and when you see them coming, HIDE! Or if there aren't any good hiding places around at the time, conjure up a jolly smile and tell a small, white, socially acceptable lie: 'I'm fine thanks.'

Keep a Journal

This can be helpful in several ways. It can be an outlet for emotions that can't be suppressed. It can clarify thoughts to put them on paper and it can ground abstract feelings and give them shape and substance. You can find yourself discovering things about the feelings and where they come from as you write. It is important to record too the positive happenings of the day that can be obscured by your general outlook and reading back over it can be a surprisingly encouraging exercise. I try to capture the ways that God is comforting me through others: once looking for these they turn up everywhere. One day during my first term at Regent, I was studying in the library, feeling distinctly wobbly and unsure of myself in this new environment. A fellow student I barely knew came up to my desk and gave me a little package of homemade chocolate chip cookies and an encouraging card, and as I wrote about it in my journal that night, it seemed to me to be a sign of God's presence with me.

It can also be a useful tool in self-discovery, highlighting patterns such as triggers that set you off into a low patch. It can illuminate the way you respond to certain situations; even times of year and weather might be significant.

Find the Thoughts that Trigger Negative Feelings

Write them down and try to answer them rationally. This afternoon I felt bad when I got home. At first I couldn't figure out why, then I pinpointed when it had started. I'd been cycling home from work in the rain. Here is how my thought ran: 'I wish I didn't have to cycle home today. I could have called Shawn and asked him to pick me up, I suppose. I wish he had thought to come and get me when he saw how rainy it was. He never thinks to do stuff like that. He doesn't really care about me. Our marriage is rubbish.' And bingo! I felt down. Once I found that little train of thoughts I reminded myself of how exhausted he usually is on Sundays with all the youth activities, how he knows that I often enjoy cycling and how many times he does think to do thoughtful things for me. After that brief conversation with myself I felt a lot better.

Look for Beauty

Beauty has a mysterious way of nourishing a famished soul. When my family and I lived in Portugal, I used to make a point of watching the sunset as often as I could. Our kitchen had a little balcony from which it was possible to climb onto the tiled roof and sit in seclusion to enjoy the show. The sun set over an estuary, beyond which was the sea, and further still the cliffs and lights of Lagos, our local town. It was achingly lovely and different every time: well done God! Chalfont St Peter maybe doesn't have the same drama, but there's nothing quite like the glory of a frosty winter morning on the common by our house, every leaf and grass sparkling white, and the sun trying to burn a hole in the mist. Now as I look around me, I find beauty in my big pink candle flickering away on the window sill, in the icon Shawn and I bought on honeymoon, in the wooden clock my grandfather made with his lathe. Try to find beauty: I promise it won't be hard if you are looking carefully. God's creation is an indescribable masterpiece. By studying it with appreciative eyes, you will find yourself drawn into worship, and out of yourself and your troubles, even if it's just momentarily. Hopefully you will be reminded of the 'things that are good, that are lovely, that are pure, that are praiseworthy...think on these things' (Philippians 4:8).

For the sake of honesty, I should mention that I have often been horribly unhappy in beautiful places too, and that sometimes it can even make it worse, because you feel you ought to be happy in such a nice place. My most extreme example of this was in a breathtakingly gorgeous botanical garden on the coast in Northern Italy, on my honeymoon no less. I think I deserve a medal for managing to be miserable under those circumstances! None of these little tips are foolproof by any means. Oh well. We can but try.

Take Care of the Basics

By this I mean the health and hygiene of your body. This means, try to get the right amount of sleep, get a bit of exercise, take regular showers, wear clean clothing, brush your teeth and eat nourishing food. To that end, I give you, free of charge, a recipe for soup invented by my friend Melissa Ong. It's really good *and* it's healthy! She made it for me while I was doing night shifts at work recently and it cheered me up a bit (I HATE night shifts).

Melissa's Yummy Soup

Fry up some bacon, onions and garlic, chopped quite fine. Add some precooked lentils, lots of chicken stock, soy sauce, chilli, carrots and broccoli (or any other veggies you have lying around in the fridge). Simmer until the smell drives you crazy and you have to eat some. Serve with chopped spring onions and grated parmesan.

Learn Relaxation Techniques

I have to say, I am a late convert to these. I had panic attacks that started when I was eleven and stopped when I was eighteen or so. I was given a relaxation tape to try to help me control them, and it was one of the funniest things ever: a creepy sounding man told me to 'clench my buttocks... clench, clench... and relax'. Creepiness aside, if you can learn to control your breathing and concentrate on the feeling of relaxation in each part of your body, it really does make you feel better. Try to allocate a room that you use each time. Allow about twenty minutes, and make everyone around aware that you are not to be disturbed. Put on some soft music, close your eyes and focus on your breathing, getting into a slow rhythm. Tense and then relax each muscle in your body in turn, then relax, focusing your mind on a mental image, such as a secluded beach, or repeating the word 'calm' to yourself. It will take time to learn this technique, but it is well worth it.

Listen to Music

Music has a mysterious ability to sooth and uplift. Compile a collection of songs you listened to when you were happy, and let them bring back positive memories and feelings, or listen to lots of calming classical music.

Play!

Release your inner child – life is too serious and the child in you doesn't want to be cooped up the whole time. I like to go to the park and swing on the swings at night. I also like play fighting with Shawn (except he is frustratingly strong and I never win). I like making cookies with no recipe even though they are not consistently edible. I like playing hide and seek with Ella the cat. I like playing 'Settlers of Catan' and 'Cranium' when friends come round for dinner. I like making potato prints and skipping and putting on silly outfits in clothes shops (yes, I am 28, and no, I am not technically deranged!). Has this list inspired you? A little?

Be Kind to Yourself

You have a lot on your plate, and you are managing to breathe in and out and in and out and sometimes do a lot more than that – that is a GREAT achievement and you should be proud of yourself. Don't expect too much of yourself. Treat yourself gently. Learn to celebrate small victories.

Don't Try This at Home Kids

We all have ways of dealing with our pain, and sometimes self-protection can go wrong and become self destruction. I recently had coffee with my friend Gemma in a posh Gerrards Cross delicatessen. Over our lattes she told me of her experiences as a self-harmer. It had begun when she was fifteen years old. She had got out of the shower one day and seen a wooden coat hanger hanging on the bathroom door. Without thinking about it, she had taken it and used it to hit her leg with some force. I asked her how she had felt afterwards, and she said, 'Calm and nothing.' She then went to find a belt with a big buckle and did it again. The next day she used a compass to scratch on her arms, and by the end of the week she was onto broken glass, which later progressed to razor blades. She explained to me how this somehow externalised her pain, and how the adrenalin produced gave her a sense of release. For others, this type of behaviour can be a form of punishment that they feel they somehow deserve. It can be a cry for help or attention. It can be calming and centring. Gemma cut and hit herself, but there are other ways that people act this behaviour out: burning, pulling out hair, breaking bones, scratching (and then blaming their innocent pet cat or a blackberry bush), or putting themselves in deliberate danger, such as walking late at night in a dodgy part of town. Obviously this list is not exhaustive but it may give you an idea of things to look out for.

If you or someone you know is self-harming please seek help. There is an excellent web site that Gemma told me about, www.busmail.org/phpBB (bus stands for Bodies under Siege, the title of the first non-medical book about this phenomenon). You could also go and see your doctor. The web site includes lots of ways to combat the impulse to harm yourself. A few of these are doing things that hurt but don't do damage, such as holding an ice cube or putting an elastic band around your wrist and flicking it. You could draw on yourself with red pen, rub moisturiser into the area you want to damage instead of attacking it, or shred a towel. I hasten to add that these are temporary measures for controlling what can be a stubborn addiction and I don't suggest them as healthy ways to deal with emotional pain if you can do without them. A parallel would be the use of methadone for heroine addicts (under medical supervision), which no one would see as an ideal, but rather as a means to an end.

There are many forms of self-destruction, or unhealthy coping strategies. Drink and drugs can provide an illusory escape, as can anonymous sexual encounters. My own battle has been with comfort eating or stringent dieting. I have sought comfort from whole loaves of bread and chocolate cake only to feel sick and empty afterwards. All of these ways of dealing with pain don't do the trick in the long run and can do real damage that will scar your life long after the depression has lifted.

Another thing that I would say, whilst on the subject of Things Not To Do, is don't make any big decisions (if you can possibly help it). When flailing around for the one key issue that is making me depressed I am always tempted to do something drastic – change jobs, move house, shave my head or get rid of all my worldly goods. It could be that there is a hinge point for how you feel, but more likely it is a whole host of factors, and any big change will add to the mess rather than sort it all out. Try to hang on until you are seeing life more clearly before making life-altering decisions.

It never helps to think of all the worse things that are happening to other people either. I used to do that a lot – and while I would on one level be thankful not to be taken hostage in Beirut (for some reason I always started with that scenario), starving in Ethiopia, lost at sea, undergoing chemotherapy etc, on another, it made me feel infinitely worse, because (a). I would realise how pathetic I was to be down for practically no reason, (b). I would over-identify with the world's suffering and get overwhelmed, and (c). I would start expecting all said scenarios to come to pass in my own life. So if you take my advice, don't do that.

Be careful of self-indulgence. There are things you can do that will make you feel much worse, and there is a strange temptation to do these in order to have a good old muddy wallow in self-pity. This could be something like pulling out a pile of letters from a boyfriend who's rejected you, putting on weepy music, or giving in to thoughts you know to be untrue such as 'I have no friends. Everything I have ever done has failed. Nothing good is ever going to happen again.' It's hard work fighting depression, and you may not have energy to fight continuously, but be on your guard against giving in too much.

Exercising Makes You Fit, Sitting Around Makes You Flabby

I started this chapter talking about discipline and choice, and it is on that same note I conclude, because it is so important that we realise we are never victims. It takes work and practice and an iron will to live with depression and not give in to the temptation to let it dominate our every move. My prayer and hope for you, and for myself, is that we will struggle and become stronger, and keep working to live the best life we can within the constraints we have been given.

Chapter 9

Spirituality

Depression strikes regardless of how robust our faith in God happens to be. If any part of us wants to believe that if a Christian gets depressed (as opposed to just miserable or low) it means they (a). are weak in their faith, (b). have unconfessed sin or (c). are one of God's least favourite creations, then those beliefs need challenging. They are simply inaccurate.

Take Elijah. Elijah was a prophet to whom God spoke regularly, leading him out of trouble, feeding him with ravens, and using him to influence the most powerful rulers of the day. He was bold and courageous, even challenging the prophets of Baal to an audacious competition to establish whose object of worship was really God (it's a good story – you can find it in 1 Kings 18). However, even he was susceptible to depression:

> *Elijah was afraid and ran for his life. When he came to Beersheba in Judah, he left his servant there, while he himself went a day's journey into the dessert. He came to a broom tree, sat down under it and prayed that he might die. 'I have had enough, Lord,' he said. 'Take my life; I am no better than my ancestors.' Then he lay down under the tree and fell asleep'*

1 Kings 19:3–5.

Charles Spurgeon preached to huge congregations in nineteenth-century London, and came to have a worldwide reputation for his powerful addresses. In his fifty-seven years he published over three thousand sermons and authored thirty-five books. All this he accomplished at great personal cost. As one of his biographers, Richard Day, wrote, 'There was one aspect of Spurgeon's life, glossed over by most of his biographers, that we must now view with utter frankness: he was frequently in the grip of terrific depression moods [sic].'[1] He struggled continually with anxiety about money, loneliness, sickness and self-doubt.

These two men were, by any account, spiritual giants, and I selected them out of a vast array of examples. Depression does not mean that you are not a 'good' Christian. It does, however, have an effect on the way that you relate to God.

An Increased Sense of the Presence of God

Depression, as a disease of the mind, colours our perception and interpretation of everything about us and within us. While depressed, we see God and our relationship to him through this lens, and it can be a dreadful distortion. On the other hand, it can bring painful clarity, for our weakness is never so fully felt as during these times, and is not our strength an illusion after all?

I have found that it is in my dark times that I have leaned most on God as my rock and my strength. When I am confident and feeling strong I have to remind myself of my need for God. When I am low I am aware of my dependence on him with every breath. My first thought in the morning will be, 'Thank you Lord that you are with me and that you will be with me through this day. Thank you that I'm not alone, and you won't let me fall.' Whilst I wouldn't want to wake up with that terrible clawing fear in my tummy, I do know that it sends me scuttling into God's arms as if my life depended on it. Contrast that with, say, this morning, when I woke up thinking of what was for breakfast (croissants and homemade marmalade as it happens: I am staying with my parents in France) and probably gave a first nod to my heavenly father sometime mid morning. It is in times of depression that we call out for God with true desperation, and when we seek him with all our hearts he promises to be found (1 Chronicles 28:9). Whatever our emotions may tell us, he is faithful and always present.

Digging a Well

A well can be a source of water even in a drought if it is deep enough to penetrate the water table that lies under the earth's surface. When we enter a spiritual drought we need a source of strength that goes far deeper than the superficialities of experience. Our faith will be severely tested, and we will have to draw on the foundations we have laid down over time, and continue to shore them up moment by moment. David Watson, a dynamic pastor and Christian leader, wrote a book during his struggle with cancer, in which he says, 'It is one thing mentally to believe the statement "God loves you". It is quite another to have a deep certainty of that within my heart and spirit. Yet that certainty is so crucial in times of crisis: a quiet, settled conviction and faith. I have found that such faith is encouraged (and it needs daily encouragement) partly by meditating on God's word of love in the scriptures, partly by the expression of God's love through caring Christian friends, but perhaps mostly by the experiencing of God's love through sensitive, joyful worship.'[2]

As Christians with depression we have a rich store to draw from in fighting our illness. As you dig into the Bible you will find all sorts of encouragement and truth to enable you to speak back to the lies invading your mind: the Word of God is described as a sword (Hebrews 4:12) and it can prove a deadly weapon against destructive thoughts. When you think, 'I am worthless and deserve to die' you can counter the thought with 'You are precious and honoured in my sight and I love you' (Isaiah 43:4). When you think 'my future is black and empty' you can chant defiantly "I know the plans

I have for you," declares the Lord, "plans to prosper and not to harm you."' (Jeremiah 29:11). If nothing your diseased mind says to you can be trusted, you can bypass it and think psalms instead.

I really don't mean to sound simplistic here; I know from experience that sometimes the lies sound completely reasonable, and it doesn't occur to you to question them. And it can get so tiring maintaining a courtroom drama in your head all day long ('Objection, your honour! The prosecution states my client is a dirty rotten sinner. This is in direct contravention of Ephesians 1:7, which states my client is forgiven.'). Some days you give in and take it all on board. But it is vital that we never cease communicating with God, even if we have nothing good to say. We have a great precedent for total honesty in prayer: the Psalms of David are full of his despair and anger. He tells God when he feels abandoned. He spews out his misery and angst and wrestles unashamedly with his doubts and fears. These psalms are a gift to those of us with depression – a prayer book we can truly relate to! They give us words when we stand before God wordless and lost in darkness, and they enable us to be before God as we are, not as we wish we were. And these psalms don't stay in the darkness: they unfailingly progress from doubt to trust, from self to God, clawing up the rock face of experience to new vistas of truth:

> *Be merciful to me, Lord, for I am faint,*
> *O Lord, heal me for my bones are in agony.*
> *My soul is in anguish.*
> *How long, O Lord, how long?*
> *I am worn out from groaning;*
> *All night I flood my bed with weeping*
> *And drench my couch with tears.*
> *My eyes grow weak with sorrow;*
> *They fail because of all my foes.*

Turn, O Lord and deliver me;
Save me because of your unfailing love.
The Lord has heard my weeping,
The Lord has heard my cry for mercy.
The Lord accepts my prayer.

Extracts from Psalm 6

Sometimes it's Hard to Be a Christian

Whilst being a Christian can be helpful in dealing with depression, it can also bring its own special complications. We have a whole added dimension to contend with. Those who don't believe in God don't give a thought to divine condemnation, eternal suffering, or failing spiritually. As Christians, this is maybe what we worry about the most. During my depression, I felt so judged by God. I believed that he frowned upon me, and was heartily disappointed and fed up with my endless failings. I believed he couldn't stand the sight of me. Here is a version of the first three verses of Psalm 23 I wrote in one such time:

The Lord doesn't love me.
I will always lack what I need.
He takes me into deserts where I am full of anguish,
And leaves me there to fend for myself.
He tests me, and puts all kinds of trials in my way.
He laughs when I fail.
The Lord is a terrible God,
He has bled my soul dry.

I did not expect answers to my prayers because I did not feel worthy, and I did not believe that God wanted anything good for me. As evidence I would point to starving children in Ethiopia, Christians imprisoned and tortured for their faith in China, any one who I assumed had called to God and been left hanging. Depression can cause us to believe the most awful lies about God.

Let me tell you about my friend Carolyn. We met on our first day of university, discovering a zillion little threads that connected us, and became friends immediately. We began to pray together regularly. When I first started at Birmingham I had a long way to go in terms of maturity and integrity – I was returning from a gap year where I had all but let go of things Christian, and was eager to find my way back. Carolyn was light years ahead and a wonderful role model for me – her relationship with God was vibrant and secure; she was unwavering in her belief and wholehearted in her desire to live in a Christ-like fashion.

While many of us waffled around wondering vaguely what to do with our post-Birmingham lives, Carolyn had set her sights on mission through music and had found herself a placement with an organisation in the Cameroon. She had sought guidance from God, found the doors opened and assumed it was where God wanted her to be.

It very soon became a nightmare. She was lonely, blighted with sickness and intensely disillusioned. The missionaries she worked with were well intentioned and very caring but their different outlook on life and at times black and white theology seemed only to add to her questions and struggles. Soon she began to feel that if Christianity equated pain, suffering and confusion, then she'd rather not follow such a God or try to convert anyone else to him. She returned to the UK quite deeply depressed, and with no desire to continue on as a follower of this God who had taken her to deepest Africa, stricken her down with disease, and forgotten her.

I met up with Carolyn in a Marylebone coffee shop a few weeks ago. She was on the way to play her oboe in her church carol service: she is still holding on to the community of faith, and is in many ways stronger than before. We talked about the effect her depression had had on her faith journey and she has come to see it as a necessary crisis – the catalyst which deconstructed her false, dogmatic beliefs, and forced her to examine the essentials in a new light. In the midst of it though, it very nearly destroyed her and any relationship that had previously existed between her and God.

Woe is Me, Miserable Sinner

People outside Christianity looking in sometimes get fixated on our concept of sin – they think it is terribly negative and destructive. Surely we should be positive about ourselves – we are after all essentially nice and good (perhaps with the exception of Hitler and his ilk). If you are a Christian, ideally the acknowledgment of sin is a relief (it fits reality rather snugly) and it leads nicely on to acceptance and gratitude of Christ's death on the cross and God's forgiveness of all we have ever done. This ideal can be shattered into pieces by depression, which fixates us on step one, and prevents us from reaching step two. We develop a sick obsession with the state of our miserable souls and never move beyond that to receiving the grace that is there for us to take hold of. Cristopher Danes, writing in the Catholic journal, *The Tablet*, says, 'During the first phase of my illness, I truly believed that I was sinful. I was certain that I was not really ill at all. I saw myself as a worthless failure and a hopeless drunk on the short road to hell. I was convinced that my failures were all my own fault... So, for a long time, I resisted my counsellors' and doctors' repeated assertions that I was truly unwell. Despite everything the counsellors said, I knew a profound truth of human existence that had been drilled into me which lies at the heart of our catechism – that we make our own moral choices.' (7 January 2006)

At times my depression has caused me to believe I am not a Christian at all. I remember a lecture at Regent on social justice, given by a man who was working with homeless drug addicts in the downtown eastside of Vancouver. I sat there burning with shame, squirming with the knowledge that I was doing NOTHING for the poor and therefore had no right to call myself a Christian. I was in tears by the end and fortunately bumped into a kindly professor who managed to reassure me.

If you find yourself dwelling on your 'manifold sins and wickedness' (thanks to the *Book of Common Prayer* for that juicy phrase) spend some time on a grace and mercy hunt through the Bible. Take a coloured pen and underline everything you find, and then concentrate on those bits until your feet are on more solid ground again. When you feel convicted of something, pray for forgiveness then let it go, whatever you feel about it. Write it on a bit of paper and flush it down the loo (if you are feeling really bad don't do this as the bulk of paper will clog the drains). God does not condemn us. He washes us white as snow (clean, new snow, not slushy three-day-old snow).

Joy

Another aspect of being a Christian that makes depression extra hard to deal with is the expectation that faith in God should make you joyful. Dr John Lockley writes, 'A depressed Christian has a double burden. Not only is he depressed but he also feels guilty because, as a Christian, he feels he is supposed to be full of joy. Joy is one of the fruits of the Spirit. So what's wrong with your spiritual life if there's no joy?'[3]

Joy is not a feeling of happiness. It is a gift from God, rooted in the reality of his presence and actions in our lives past and present, and an expectation of the same in our future. Peterson explains, 'joy is not dependent on our good luck in escaping hardship. It is not dependent on our good health and avoiding pain. Christian joy is actual in the midst of pain, suffering, loneliness and misfortune.'[4] When you are depressed, there are occasional touches of joy, like feeling the whisper of a winter sun on your cheek. But most of the time, it is hidden far behind the banks of black cumulonimbus. THIS IS NOT YOUR FAULT! (Isn't it great how using upper case letters is like shouting?) Being depressed means you are not seeing life in its true perspective, and you will genuinely believe things that are false. You will not have a sure and certain hope for the future, and you will not (in all likelihood) believe that God is with you and loves you. This does not mean you are a lesser Christian. It is symptomatic of your illness. The joy will return when you get well, because it is a natural consequence of Christian discipleship: 'it is what comes to us when we are walking in the way of faith and obedience.'[5]

An Enemy

I don't want to give the devil much airtime but I would like to make one quick point about him. The Bible is clear that we have a spiritual battle on our hands at all times, and there is a key player to watch out for: 'Your enemy the devil prowls around like a roaring lion looking for someone to devour' (1 Peter 5:8). A lion will not have a qualm about ripping apart an injured kudu – when we're depressed we are vulnerable in the same way, and we should be aware of that reality. Satan will strike us when we are weak and delight in doing so. That is not to say we should be afraid. Rather we should be prepared to fight back, arm ourselves with truth, ask others to pray for us, and keep our wits about us.

Please don't hear me say that depression is the devil taking over our minds – I don't mean that at all. What I mean is that Satan is a nasty reality and he will try to take advantage of us when we're down.[6]

Into the Breach, Dear Friends

When we crumble spiritually we need others around us to have faith on our behalf, to step into the breach and keep the flood waters out. With apologies to the Amalekites, I love the story of their defeat in Exodus. It kind of illustrates what I want to say here. While the Israelites are doing battle, Moses stands on top of the hill holding up the staff of God (whatever that was). As long as he holds it up, his team wins, but when he lowers it, the opposition draws ahead. As the day goes by, he gets tired, so Aaron and Hur, who are with him, sit him on a rock and they hold his arms up for him (Exodus 17:8–13). We all need our Aarons and Hurs to hold our arms up sometimes. This is what it means to be in the family of God, and it's OK to admit we don't have the strength to do it ourselves.

As well as friends, we need God to sustain us. He keeps faith even when we don't. He knows about depression more than any psychiatrist because he knows us inside out – all our sickness and weakness and broken bits are old news to him. Our relationship with him is not equal: he goes a lot further than half way to make sure we meet. So don't panic if your depression causes you to feel that you can't relate to God, don't like him, can't pray, hate church, can't worship, don't feel joyful, feel too evil to be forgiven, can't accept grace... This is your depression speaking, not you, and God knows that.

I would like to pray for you, if you don't mind.

> *Dear Lord,*
> *I know that your heart breaks with sorrow to see your creation crippled with so much pain and suffering. Thank you that you are with us. You are with us even when depression takes over our minds and blinkers our eyes and stops us from being able to feel or understand your love. Lord, please comfort all those bound up in the chains of despair. Please carry them, and sustain them and break through their darkness. Give them courage to keep breathing in and out, and to keep fighting the lies that fill their minds. Lord give them hope that one day you will redeem their experience, that it won't be wasted. I pray that you will surround them with Christian*

brothers and sisters to hold up their arms. You are good, loving, merciful, faithful, eternal. These things are true, and we thank you for them.
Amen.

Chapter 10

Church

When I was three, my father became a curate at St Mary's, Upton. By all accounts it was a flourishing, lively and loving church to be a part of. My own memories consist of rushing up and down the red-carpeted-isles waiting for Dad to de-robe at the end of the Sunday morning service, learning about Noah's ark and Joseph's snazzy coat on one of those fuzzy-felt boards, and idolising the youth group who came regularly to our house and patiently played with us. When we moved to Portugal our church attendance as a family became sporadic; when we did go it would either be to a stodgy Southern Baptist church run by American missionaries, or to a wild Pentecostal gathering, where choruses were sung 140 times each and prayers were drowned out in increasingly loud and fervent cries of 'amen, amen, AMEN!' As children we thought this was a riot, and would join in with gusto before collapsing in giggles behind the pew.

We always had some sort of gathering with a spiritual focus on Sundays however, with whoever was staying at Cruzinha at the time and wanted to attend. In the warmer weather this would be outside under the rubber tree. I suppose it usually had the elements of a conventional service; singing, Bible reading, a talk, prayer, sometimes communion, but it felt very 'unreligious' for want of a better word.

Every few years we returned to the UK for Mum and Dad's dutiful tour of the Supporting Churches. We trooped around the country as a family visiting a selection of these, one Sunday apiece. We children would stand gauchely at the front, secretly feeling a bit like celebrities and rather proud of our exotic lives, and then attend a tea/lunch/supper buffet and answer the inevitable questions: 'Do you like Portugal or England better?' (Portugal, but England is nice too) 'What is it like living near the beach?' (Very nice, thank you).

Actually, the beach was the backdrop for my first dramatic encounter with God, at the age of eleven. I had been going through a precociously rocky patch, and was not very enamoured with all things Christian – family prayer times were 'icky' and the Bible was boring – when some students came to stay and took me under their wing. They were en route to a big Christian gathering in Lisbon, and were the most animated Christians I had yet encountered. One afternoon we went to Meia Praia, a long, flat postcard-pretty beach nearby, and they prayed for me to be filled with the Holy Spirit. What followed took me completely by surprise: I laughed, prayed in tongues, and felt an incredible sense of God's love and light around me and on me.

At boarding school, there were chapel services four times a week. Occasionally I would feel uplifted by the words of a hymn or challenged by a guest speaker's message, but most often it was a bit of an ordeal. At university and at Regent, I was up to my neck in 'Christian activities' and commitments, but still never really became rooted in a local church.

A year and a half ago, Shawn and I arrived in England and became a part of St James' Church. This is my first genuine experience of church membership, and it has been a kind of enlightenment. I feel so blessed to have found a church home with such energy, wise and gifted leadership, and creative ministry. I am beginning to see why God thinks the church is such a good idea.

Why is it such a hard place to be sometimes?

I confess I have at times found Psalm 27:4 a bit hard to relate to:

One thing I ask of the Lord,
This is what I seek:
That I may dwell in the house of the Lord
All the days of my life.

What, live in church? My whole life? No thank you! I hope that by giving you a potted history of my church experience that response might seem less shocking, although my bet is I am not the only one to feel that way. My struggles with church have been partly due to my particular story, and partly to do with my depression. Let me elaborate.

While I had plenty of exposure to many shapes and sizes of church, this exposure was always brief and superficial. I would attend one or two services and form an impression, or a judgment, based on the style of the music or the decorations on the wall. Often I would feel bored and/or uncomfortable with the proceedings, and so I gradually formed the opinion that I did not fit into church culture. This opinion was reinforced by the fact that none of my significant encounters with God happened in a formal church setting.

Going to school chapel was a strange experience. The great majority of those singing the hymns, incanting the prayers, and reading the Bible passages, had no belief in God and no desire to be there. It was pure ceremony, and it was hard to participate in any sort of meaningful way.

Later on, church attendance seemed like one more duty in a busy schedule. To my husband's horror, I even stopped going for a few months when we were first married. It fell too low down on the priority list and there were too many other elements in my life to make it feasible, or so I felt at the time. In short, although I was a committed member of the body of Christ at large, I resisted becoming a member of a specific limb of that body, finding the thought boring, intimidating, and generally pointless.

Being Depressed in Church

My times of depression have doubtless coloured my experiences of church. Here are some reasons I think church can be a particularly difficult place to be when you are low. Firstly, there is a lingering suspicion amongst Christians in general that if you are a Christian you really shouldn't be depressed in the first place. Obviously, at church you come across Christians en masse, and this attitude can be sensed pervading the atmosphere like mustard gas, in a million invisible molecules. A depressed person has antennae for disapproval and judgment more sensitive than you'd think possible, and so this does not go unnoticed.

Secondly, church services can be very upbeat and focused on those things about the Christian faith that are hopeful and victorious. As everyone sings joyfully the joyful words of the songs and you try to wobble along with them, you feel more and more hypocritical and alienated. There is very little you can grab onto with conviction, so the sense of dislocation is magnified.

Thirdly, church can be a hard place for the depressed person because it has its unspoken codes of behaviour. We come to meet with God and each other, and we strive for authenticity in that, and yet there are rigid guidelines for what is appropriate and what is not. The pressure to keep a brave face on is very real, and yet it feels fake and deceptive to do so. It would be self-indulgent to let it all hang out, and after all we are there to focus on God not ourselves. Even so, the tension exists, and makes it hard to want to attend.

Fourthly, church can be a bit of a fishbowl, where you and your problems are visible to a number of people you may not even know very well. This is humbling and uncomfortable, and really you might prefer to hide away and only let a couple of people you trust in on the messy situation. Even if you are not depressed, the mingling bit at the end of services can be a bit of an endurance test – lots of small talk and awkward heartiness and crinkly Christian smiles all round.

What Can Be Done?

I really don't think that it is an option to simply opt out of church membership if you are going through depression. And it is not an option for churches to neglect or exclude gloomy people. So what is to be done? And what is already being done?

A Vision

Here is a fictional scenario to ponder. I wake up at 5 a.m. My first sensation is a sinking in my stomach and a tight band around my head. I cast around for reasons to keep going, and then I realise: it's Sunday! Today is Church Day. A tentative light breaks into my mind and I decide today will be worth living. I am in bed until nine, when I get up to answer the phone. It is my house group leader phoning to see if she can give me a lift, as she knows how hard it can be for me to get going and how it can feel walking into church alone.

I cry while I dress, weep over my cereal and sob as I brush my teeth. By the time my lift arrives my eyes are red and puffy. If someone asks how I am they will only have to look at me to know the answer. Usually I would have to soak my face with cold water and apply some emergency make up, but today I will be among friends and it doesn't matter if I look how I feel.

When I arrive I am greeted by a couple of friends who give me big, wordless hugs and I go with them into the sanctuary. In the service I am reassured of God's love and, although I do not feel his presence especially, I am comforted by the truth of his word. I continue to cry on and off, but no one makes me feel weird or out of place. At the end a few people gather round me and pray. Then I am invited to lunch, even though I tell them I am a misery guts and will ruin their fun.

Before I go home I have several offers of help and support for the following week. One person is going to phone me each morning at seven to get me out of bed. I am having dinner with someone and going to the cinema with someone else. One kind person is coming round to help me with the cleaning. I am not alone. I am not going to fall through the cracks. I am part of God's family and they are going to look after me.

Signs of Hope:

Community

Writing that last bit, I realise that what I most need when I am depressed, is for the church to be a community. The good news is that the church is by its very nature a community. It is not a question of creating it, more of recognising it for what it already is and finding one's place within it. No church is going to be ideal – there is no such thing. But we are a family, with a family's responsibilities to one another. This means that as a depressed person I must resist the temptation to withdraw and stay where the family can reach me and I can reach them. I am going to quote my mum on this subject as she has some good stuff to say on this:

> We do not need to create communities; rather, we need to identify and describe those we already belong to...genuine community can be created with people of similar, different, or indeed no particular beliefs. It begins with inclusion; it involves love, acceptance and forgiveness, and it depends on a commitment to transparent relationships and self-giving hospitality... Unconditional welcome is God's unreserved gift to us. We are not at liberty to introduce a different set of rules for those who arrive on our doorstep.[1]

Church is about far more than the Sunday service

component. We are groups of people dedicated to sharing life with one another. This means meals together, celebrations and grief, milestones and a communal history. It means welcoming each other into our homes, sharing our possessions and praying for one another. In a large church like St James (we have in the realm of one thousand members) it is not practical to share life with every single person, so smaller groups are formed. At this point a short tribute is merited to the house group I am currently a part of. We are a group of fourteen or so women, and we meet on Thursday mornings. When I first joined I felt like a chicken in a flock of swans: these women are sophisticated, glamorous, and well into the children phase of life. I am as yet childless, and no one has ever called me glamorous, as I am a bit scruffy, buy my clothes from charity shops, and sometimes forget to brush my hair (Mascara? What's that?). So I wondered if I would fit in. Well, the news is, I do! I have seen this community thing work out first hand, as more babies have been born, parents have died, marriages have struggled, jobs have come and gone, and these women have supported and loved each other throughout, in extremely tangible ways. And when I have wondered if I was falling into depression again, I have been able to share my fears and be prayed for without fear of rejection or scorn.

Leadership

Leaders have an awesome responsibility for shaping the direction and setting the tone for their churches. A leader who frowns upon those who show weakness will convey this attitude to the community and it will become a hostile and unsafe environment for those who are depressed. Conversely, those who believe in unconditional acceptance and grace will be a great force for good. This attitude shows not only through what they say from up front, but through the way they interact with their 'flock' and the provision they make for pastoral care in their church. Williams, Richards and

Whitton write, 'For our churches to be really effective in supporting those with mental health difficulties, we need to establish a culture where everyone in the local church knows that it is acceptable to have problems from time to time, and that the church as a whole – and especially its leadership – is there to support church members during these times as well as times of success. Ideally this work in agenda-setting needs to begin quite some time before an individual develops mental illness rather than in response to it.'[2]

Could I be so bold as to make a couple of suggestions for the church leaders who may be reading this? Examine your own attitudes to depression. Search your heart for prejudice and fear, and tackle them head on. If you have unresolved personal issues in this area, seek help. As a church leader you are just as likely to have depression as anyone else – there is no shame in admitting this.

Educate yourself. Depression is widespread, and I can almost guarantee that if you have a congregation of more than five people, someone under your care is going to be suffering now or in the future from this condition.

Find out what the resources are in your area in terms of counselling and support groups. There will be cases that call for referrals to those who have professional capabilities and it is right and good to work in conjunction with these people.

Train up lay pastoral workers to step up when needed. Make sure they are vetted for suitability and are not wanting to care for others out of a desperation to meet their own needs. Ensure that they value confidentiality and know to look for signs of serious suicidal intent and mental illness such as schizophrenia.

I really hope I don't sound bossy and prescriptive here: it is a terribly hard job to lead a church, and I thankfully am not in that position so it's easy for me to sit and pontificate. Thank you for the job that you do, and God bless you as you do it.

Heading in the Right Direction

In my twenty-eight years I have seen suffering, not only depression, but suffering of all kinds handled both badly and extremely well, and I do believe that things are generally getting better in this respect. Two situations stand out: one was an award winning success, another was really well meant, and actually pretty humorous (which is the real reason I am including it if I'm honest!).

While it is right to focus on God in worship and adoration when we come together as Christians, there also needs to be space and time for authentic grappling with current reality: the ever-present tension of the 'now but not yet' Kingdom of God on earth. The chapel coordinator while I was at Regent was extremely gifted at orchestrating services that touched on the whole spectrum of human experience. One that I remember in particular was the morning that the World Trade Centre towers were destroyed by terrorists. Regent has a large proportion of students from the US and many knew of people who may have been in the danger zone. Grief was mixed with anger which added to shock and disbelief and all of this and more was brought to our time of weekly worship. Microphones were set up all around the auditorium and a dialogue with each other and God was begun in amongst prayer, scripture and song. It was a profound and moving time that had a lasting impact on many of us and set the tone for the community's processing of the events.

Some churches, and they deserve credit for this, really do try. If they happen to miss the mark it is certainly not intentional. One Sunday I was visiting a friend's church and found myself weeping at the communion rail. I had been sitting towards the back of the church and decided that the long walk back up the aisle with all eyes on me, imaginations working overtime, would not be the best idea ('Has she had a spat with her husband? Maybe she has cancer? etc). Thankfully there was a side door I could escape through. I had not reckoned on **THE PRAYER MINISTRY TEAM** in my cunning plan. As the two dear old ladies saw me approach, there was a visible flutter of excitement, as a real crying person came needing their services! Well, I thought to myself, a person can always do with prayer. The next few moments were painful for both me and the lady attending to me. Bear in mind that we were in the main body of the sanctuary, albeit slightly off to the side behind a pillar, the music group were doing their thing, the sweet ladies no longer had optimum hearing abilities and I did not have a very specific problem. Imagine the scene:

'What's the matter? What would you like prayer about?' (I have been claimed by the one in the green cardigan, who is patting my arm in glee – some real ministry to be done at last!)

'I am just feeling a bit low...'

'What can I pray for you about dear?' (Concern and kindness beaming from behind thick, brown-rimmed spectacles.)

(Leaning in and speaking directly into her ear) 'I am feeling low. Could you pray for peace.'

'You're feeling so...? So, what, dear?'

'LOW. NOT 'SO' ANYTHING. LOW.'

'I see.' (Not seeing. And I think I may have overdone the shouting and offended her. Gosh, this is awkward. I just wanted to get out of the side door and now I have hurt and confused a pray-er. It's all going horribly wrong.)

You get the idea. By the time I got out to the graveyard I was seeing the funny side and she had actually managed to make me feel significantly better, if not in the way she intended!

Hooray for the Church!

I would like to conclude this chapter by extolling the glories of the church. In this day and age one hears all sorts of slander and scathing critiques hurled in its direction, to the point where you feel you almost need a dozen qualifying statements whenever you mention your own commitment to the institution. We take blame for all sorts of ills perpetuated in the crusades, against women, for the occasional hypocrisy of our most public leadership (OK, fairly frequent hypocrisy) and so on. Criticism doesn't only come from the 'outside' – many Christians, and I shamefully include myself in this, are happy to sit around pulling apart the way we do things and the way we don't do things and who does what and when and where and why they shouldn't or should, and how great things would be if they were all completely different. The point is this: in some mysterious and beautiful way, we the church, the body of those who believe in the resurrected Jesus Christ, are nothing less than his cherished bride. If God cherishes us, we should cherish ourselves, as a natural part of our worship to him.

Above all, it is a great privilege to be a part of the church. Bonhoeffer, in his book *Life Together* gives a strong reminder of the gift it is to enjoy fellowship with other believers, in a life lived predominantly in the 'thick of foes'. He writes that 'the physical presence of other Christians is a source of incomparable joy and strength to the believer' and exhorts, 'Let him who until now has had the privilege of living a common Christian life with other Christians praise God's grace from the bottom of his heart. Let him thank God on his knees and declare: It is grace, nothing but grace that we are allowed to live in community with Christian brethren.'[3]

As Christians, we have a ready-made worldwide family. This is not just a concept, it is a reality. We have a place we belong, people we belong to, and we are not alone.

I believe in...the holy Catholic Church; the Communion of Saints; the Forgiveness of sins; The Resurrection of the body, and the life everlasting. Amen.[4]

Chapter 11

Story

No one really wants to believe that there is no meaning to their life, that their life does not connect to anyone else's, that there is no discernable shape in the patchwork of happenings. We all want a story and we want our story to be a part of a greater story.

There are three kinds of story I want to look at in this chapter. The first kind is personal narrative, the stories we tell about our own lives. The second is fiction, the stories we read and hear that become a metaphor for our experiences. The third is the great meta-narrative of God's story in which we can find our own place.

All three layers of story form a frame around the window of our perception. In the midst of depression we can forget that this frame exists. I think that there are many ways in which stories can break down our isolation and remind us of a greater purpose and shape to our lives and this is why I thought it important to have a chapter on story in a book about depression.

Personal Narrative

Mr J. L. B. Maketoni was always prepared to listen to stories about Obed Ramotswe, although he had heard them all from Mma Ramotswe many times over. He had heard the story of how Obed Ramotswe had met Seretse Khama once when he had come to Mochudi and had shaken the great man's hand. He had heard the story of his hat, and how it had once been left near the

Kgotsa and carefully placed on a wall where he might find it again. He had also heard about how the hat had been blown off his head once in a storm, and had ended up in a tree. There were many such stories, and he understood just how important they were, and listened with patience and with respect. A life without stories would be no life at all. And stories bound us, did they not, one to another, the living to the dead, people to animals, people to the land?[1]

One of the first classes I took at Regent College was 'The Christian Life'. It involved an hour and a half lecture and an hour and a half of time spent in a 'Community Group' each week. Our first assignment was to write our life story, which we then read out to the group. It was an interesting exercise, and helpful in several ways. On a personal level, it enabled us to look at our lives thus far from a step away, to assess where things had got to and where they had come from. As we wrote we realised what and who had been important in directing our steps, and how very little seemed pointless or wasted. If you haven't done this before I can recommend it.

As a group of people who had only just met, it was a fast track to intimacy and connectedness. We had knowledge of each other's histories that would have taken years to garner under normal circumstances. We discovered commonalities and parallels that may never have come to light. We had made ourselves vulnerable and we had no choice but to trust the group with the information we had shared.

When you tell someone your story you are creating a bridge between you that crosses the divide and connects you to another. So much of the experience of being human is shared. When we begin to exchange narratives we catch ourselves exclaiming, 'Me too!' surprised as though some great coincidence had been stumbled upon. This shared humanity transcends gender, age, nationality, religion. We all experience love, loss, need, sorrow, joy. To discover this is to turn on the light in a dark, empty room, only to find it's a surprise party and there are friends hiding behind all the furniture ready to jump out and celebrate your birthday. Telling our stories and hearing those of others illuminates the company you have surrounding you.

Depression makes the divide even greater, so we are even more in need of these bridges. People need a way to reach us – they can't climb into our heads and read our thoughts: we must take the risk to venture out and put words to our experience. It will be good for us, and good for them. Our stories will provide the framework for them to build an understanding of a condition that may be entirely foreign to them. And as they gain understanding, so we gain a companion in the darkness. Sharing stories can be powerfully healing.

Andrew Solomon tells of a Cambodian woman, Phaly Nuon, who has a centre for depressed women in Phnom Penh that has seen phenomenal success in rehabilitating those who have been given up on by all others. Part of her approach is in getting the women to tell their stories. She says this:

> [they] begin to talk together, and bit by bit they learn to trust one another, and by the end of it all, they have learned how to make friends, so that they will never have to be lonely and so alone again. Their stories, which they have told to no one but me – they begin to tell those stories to one another.[2]

Sometimes telling our stories is something we do for ourselves. It is a form of therapy – giving us the chance to polish and tidy and present our lives in an acceptable fashion. But sometimes we do it for others. Our stories can be a beacon of hope to those doing battle with similar foes, and they might take courage from our experience. Anne Lamott, in her book on writing, *Bird by Bird*, urges her reader, 'If you are no longer wracked or in bondage to a person or a way of life, tell your story. Risk freeing someone else.'[3] She likens life to a recycling centre, in which all of human experience is used and reused, so that humans essentially share all the same dramas and concerns and are thus able to relate to one another in a profound way.[4] If I have been able to make one person feel less isolated then any struggle I have gone through in telling my story, it will have been worth it.

When we craft a story about something that's happened to us, we are doing just that: crafting. We are selecting and arranging and organising, choosing to include or exclude, emphasise or brush over certain details. We may do this very differently depending on our mood or who we are talking to. In the midst of depression we will probably see things in pretty dire terms – a sorry tale of failure and missed opportunity. It can be helpful to get some objective observer to get the facts straight and remind us of another perspective. However we tell it, we live life as story:

> *Stories and storytelling are integral to being human. Within the privacy of our own heads we experience life as a series of interrelated stories, which when collected together become the anthology of our personal experience. These are genuine narratives, constructions that link factual events and episodes of emotional significance. As we tell ourselves these stories we give important people, places and events their own special meaning.[5]*

Of course it is always disastrously possible to fabricate. The most audacious example of a falsified life story that I have encountered was a family who lived near us in Portugal: a mother, father and son. The mother was my geography teacher and the father ran a riding school. Harry, the son, was in my class, and we sometimes played together after school. Well, one day they were there, the next they had gone, and the day after that they were in the papers. Turns out, Harry had been stolen from America from his true mother by the dad, who had been refused custody. The mum, my geography teacher, was his girlfriend. They had made-up names, made-up histories and made-up relationships. It was quite the scandal.

Most of us are not such pathological liars, but we are all capable of tweaking the truth. Some of the things we have done or had done to us are very uncomfortable, ugly even, and we'd prefer they were not a part of the story. The thing is, the more honest we are able to be, the more we gain self-understanding and learn from our mistakes.

Personal stories are of immense importance in understanding the roots of depression in our lives. Whybrow writes, 'the only way to understand what has the power to kindle and precipitate a depression is to know the personal story that lies behind the experience and the illness.'[6] To tell our story, we must first know what it is. We must familiarise ourselves with the ins and outs, the twists and turns. We must seek to draw order out of the swirling images.

Sometimes we are told stories about ourselves that we accept and take on as our own when we shouldn't, because they are not true, and they harm us. The danger of these stories is that we can start to live inside them, making them eventually into truth. The key to the lock of some people's depression is weeding out these stories and retelling them. The essential story of our true identity is told by Brent Curtis and John Eldridge as follows:

The gospel says that we, who are God's beloved, created a cosmic crisis. It says we, too, were stolen from our True Love and that he launched the greatest campaign in the history of the world to get us back. God created us for intimacy with him. When we turned our back on him he promised to come for us. He sent personal messengers; he used beauty and affliction to recapture our hearts. After all else failed, he conceived the most daring of plans. Under the cover of night he stole into the enemy's camp incognito, the Ancient of Days disguised as a new born.[7]

We are God's beloved. If we understand ourselves as people who are loved more than life itself, we will have the clarity to discard any narrative that says otherwise.

Fiction

You do not lose yourself in the best stories. Rather you find yourself, or at least a potential self.[8]

While we were children, my family had a bedtime routine of a story, a song and a pray. We would riot if we were put to bed without it! The best bit for me was the story. I would sit enthralled in my jammies, snuggled up next to Mum as she took us through some of the best children's literature ever created. We journeyed to Narnia, met the Fossil girls, discovered the Secret Garden, rode the Little White Horse. However much she read was never quite enough, even when we made her carry on until her voice gave out! These stories came to be homes away from homes, places I could escape to when my own life was less than appealing. They gave me ideals to aspire to, standards for comparison – a sort of reality check at times. When I was picked on or excluded at school, I had literary friends who had faced the same challenges and I knew how they had fared. When I felt misunderstood by my family, hosts of paper people came to mind who had too. They gave me ideas for coping. They made me feel like a heroine in my own story. Fiction, John Gardener claims, '...clarifies life, establishes models of human action, casts nets towards the future, carefully judges our right and wrong directions, celebrates and mourns... it designs visions worth trying to make facts.'[9]

I once had a rather confrontational discussion with a man on a ferry about whether fiction was a waste of time. He believed it was. He himself only read instructional books on the spiritual life. If I remember rightly, my response to this opinion was more heated than was polite in a conversation with a stranger. Shawn was a bit embarrassed to be associated with me on that occasion! The truth is, I feel very strongly that stories contribute to a rich inner life just as much as this man's worthy 'instructional' reading matter. When the ferry docked and we disembarked I like to think he went straight to the nearest bookshop to buy *Anna Karenina* or *Birdsong*, convinced by my sound and impassioned reasoning, because I am sure this would have improved his circumscribed life immensely!

Sometimes fiction is just a means of good old escapism. A novel with a tight plot, convincing characterisation and an eloquent turn of expression can provide blessed relief from life with depression. You really can get lost in the print for a while. And when things look impossibly bleak from where we stand, it is comforting to sink into a fantasy where 'the battle goes ultimately to the good, who live happily ever after, and where in the long run everybody, good and evil alike, becomes known by his true name'.[10]

If there was any need to provide evidence for the hunger for stories, we need look no further than the daily soaps on television. My patients at work spend huge proportions of their time with us wrapped up in the fictional lives of the residents of Ramsey Street, Emmerdale and Albert Square. Try to interrupt their daily fix and they respond with the frenzied desperation of addicts gone 'cold-turkey'. They are away from home and family, uncertain of the future of their health, struck down periodically by seizures, and they need their soaps to take them into another world. I should say that I generally disapprove of these programmes and am not by any means endorsing the habit of ordering your life around television scheduling!

God's Story

It seems that an integral part of the human condition is the propensity to ask questions about the nature of life and the world. We do not simply accept things as the way they are, but we search hungrily for the answers to the big, mysterious 'whys?': Why are we here? Why is there suffering? Why do we die, and what happens then? Northrop Frye observes 'Man lives, not nakedly in nature, like the animals, but within a mythological universe, a body of assumptions and beliefs developed from his existential concerns.'[11] As a Christian, I take issue with his conclusion that these assumptions and beliefs emanate from our concerns: rather I think that they are a real part of the fabric of the universe – a sense of truth that we have as beings made in the image of God. But I agree that all of us inhabit a meta-narrative – even if that narrative is that there are no discernable narratives.

Donald Miller, an American author and speaker who I have only recently discovered, explores how the essential elements of story seem to emanate from the greatest story of all – God's story of creation and redemption. These elements, as he learned in his college literature class, are setting, conflict, climax and resolution. His decision to accept the validity of Christianity came from a realisation that there was a fundamental reason for why these elements, together forming the thing we call story, resonate so profoundly with all human beings: they derive from this one grand meta-narrative. And each of us has our own niche in this story. Setting: wherever we are. Conflict: our sin which separates us from God. Climax: what will we decide to do about this separation? Resolution: 'Christian spirituality offered a resolution, the resolution of forgiveness and a home in the afterlife...I wanted desperately to believe it. It felt as though my soul were designed to live the story Christian spirituality was telling. I felt like my soul wanted to be forgiven. I wanted the resolution God was offering.'[12]

We only really find peace in our identity once we locate our place in the mega story, the story in which all other stories are cocooned. Christians sometimes try to extract principles and truths and theologies from the scriptures, in order to fit them round their lives, as though putting on a corset. Eugene Peterson, a pastor, biblical scholar and teacher, argues that this is not the gospel way: the gospel way is story, and 'story isn't imposed on our lives; it invites us into its life'.[13] Christians indwell this story, looking through it, rather than at it. Everything that happens to us is interpreted in the light of knowing that mankind is fallen, that redemption is possible and that Jesus will eventually return and put all things right. This enables us to make sense of why things are the way they are and we seek to live in the world in accordance with the story. Newbigin states, 'History... is not the story of the development of forces immanent within history; it is a matter of the promise of God.'[14] We must hold on to that truth when we are depressed. God will not abandon us – he keeps his promises, and he holds all of history in his hands. We are a part of that history, and our story is a part of his story.

Chapter 12

Healing

It was a hazy, September afternoon. I went straight from class to the bus stop to catch the number 17 bus to downtown Vancouver, where I would change by the Bay department store and get the 250 out to West Van along Marine Drive. I kept my eyes down and walked fast, hoping I wouldn't see anyone I knew. This was a highly covert mission: my first appointment with a 'shrink' and I felt ambivalent about the exercise to say the least.

To back track: the idea of talk-therapy had first come across my radar some three years previously. A wise friend had suggested that I might want to consider counselling or psychotherapy, and much as I respected her advice in general, this particular nugget received the inner response, 'Yeah, like that's going to happen!' My own great wisdom had come up with the following foolproof reasons for not going down that particular path:

1. When I talk in depth to anyone about my depression and its possible causes I feel significantly worse, *ergo* talking makes me feel worse, *ergo* I really don't want to do it on a regular basis, and if I do it will do more harm than good.
2. What if people find out I have had counselling? They will think I am a nutter and never look at me in the same way again.
3. I know people who have real problems – broken families, sexual assault, chronic illness. I do not deserve the attention of a professional. I should be able to manage on my own.

4. If I spend time focusing on myself and my problems I will become self-absorbed and navel-gazing. I will be insufferable and no one will like me anymore.

5. Everyone has something hard to deal with in life. You cannot expect perfect happiness. Depression is the 'thorn in my side' and an attitude of stoic endurance will eventually make me a stronger person, as well as very holy!

6. Maybe the depression will go away by itself and not come back. My life might take a turn for the better and I will look back one day and realise that being low is a thing of the past.

The episodes of depression continued and the advice to seek professional help began to crop up on a regular basis. When I moved to Canada some of my personal prejudice was eroded by living in a culture where people see their counsellor like they see their dentist: as often as it takes to deal with the pain, and with no song and dance about whether it is necessary/appropriate or not (try applying some of the reasons above to a cavity...).

Predictably enough, by about the middle of October I was depressed again. One evening I sat crying in a friend's car outside my house as she was dropping me off. She listened to my jumbled account of the possible reasons I could be crying on that particular occasion, before the by-now-familiar suggestion of seeing a counsellor was presented to me. The difference was, she had someone in mind, a close friend of hers who she thought incredibly highly of both professionally, personally, and who had helped numerous people get back on their emotional feet. In reply I wheeled out reason number 3, that my problems did not merit the attentions of such a fine psychiatrist, thinking she would see the sense in what I said and drop the matter. Instead she said, 'You could live perfectly well with a broken arm too. But if you had the chance to fix it, your life would be better for it, and you'd have no qualms about taking the chance would you?' I thought about this over the next few weeks. Maybe I wasn't hospitalised for a breakdown, but my depression was definitely debilitating in its own small way. Could this be the justification I needed for getting help? Did I really believe that it could be helped? I almost didn't dare to hope it could. By Christmas I had made an appointment.

Enter my parents. They too had a definitive list of reasons why Seeing a Counsellor Is a Bad Idea, a pretty similar list to mine. Bear in mind that I still thought the list was very impressive. When I told them, while home for the holidays, about my appointment, they quickly convinced me that I should cancel it forthwith, which I did. I love my parents very much and it has taken me a long time to realise that now I am an adult their opinions and advice are just that: opinions and advice. They would be the first to agree with that. However, at that point their word was law to me, and I am not a natural law-breaker.

The depression dragged on. Back in Vancouver, I began to reach the end of my tolerance, and while I still felt that the likelihood of getting better by talking about it was slim, it was something proactive that I could do at least. I say I am not a natural law-breaker, but maybe a more accurate statement would be, 'I don't like getting caught breaking the law.' So I made another appointment, but kept it a secret this time.

After a year, I was outed. My psychiatrist, Dr R., happened to co-own a campervan with a friend, in which they travel up the sunshine coast for several weeks each summer. My parents were going to join them for a few days on a visit to Canada and wanted me to come along. Dr R. and I both felt this would be very awkward while we were seeing each other on a client/psychiatrist basis, but couldn't think of a convincing cover story about why I couldn't go. So I told them. My mum and dad are wonderful. While this news was hard for them, they listened carefully, respected my decision and eventually came on board with their support and approval. They are now advocates of both counselling and medication where appropriate.

I will always be indebted to Dr R. I could not have hoped for a more intelligent, experienced, spiritually mature human being to take my hand and lead me (drag me?) down a path towards wholeness and self-knowledge. She was unstintingly incisive in her observations, and did not tolerate either laziness or lies. She was patient and clear with me when I questioned her almost weekly about what we were achieving and why it was worth my time and hers. Her office, with its olive-green walls, beige cord sofa and tastefully arranged artefacts, plants and pictures became the setting for immense inner drama. During the first session she said there would be times I would regard her with murderous intent, other times I would want to marry her – she was right! I once actually *growled* at her! (She was very pleased by this for it showed I was making progress in getting in touch with my anger.)

Three years later, I knew it was the best investment I could have made. As the dust has settled, and the ups and downs of life have continued, I am able to see the things that have happened to me as a result of all this talking. I now know when I am angry. I know because my back will get tense and my fists will clench and my heart will go faster. I know now that this is not the end of the world and no one will necessarily die as a result of this feeling I have. I have laid certain experiences to rest. I have faced them head on, forgiven myself and the others involved, and identified the triggers that take me right back there. I have decided to move on and let them go. I have understood that all we have to offer God is our weakness and our poverty and he is able to take this meagre gift and turn it into a thing of beauty. We can only be real before him. I am made up of positive and negative feelings and have to accept that both are a part of me. I have learnt that I, and only I, am responsible for how I behave.

Can You Get Better?

I have come to believe that depression is an illness for which there is hope of a cure. The means are many: among them, talk-therapy, medication, love... Andrew Solomon writes, 'By themselves pills are a weak poison, love a blunt knife, insight a rope that snaps under too much strain. With the lot of them, if you are lucky, you can save the tree from the vine.'[1]

It is easy to lose hope in the midst of a depression, and to feel that life is not ever going to look bright again. But help is at hand, and all is not lost! Many, including me, are living above ground once again, and you can too. Dorothy Rowe emphatically states that, 'The key to your prison of depression is within your grasp.'[2] Do you dare believe that?

Do You Want To?

Whichever means you decide to pursue to get better, a decision needs to be made at the outset that you want to get better. There are all sorts of reasons why we might not want to, as strange as that might seem. Depression can become an ingrained part of our identity, part of the very fabric of who we are. It can be a handy excuse for not taking any risks, a scape-goat for the lack of substance in our lives. It can draw the attention and sympathy of others, and we can be fearful of losing that if we were well. Any kind of change is threatening and scary, even a positive change, and to go from being a depressed person to someone who is not depressed is definitely a change. We can protect ourselves from disappointment by expecting the worst, and hide away from the risk that things really can't get better. We need to search inside for any of these reasons lurking around and oust them before any progress can be made.

Talk-Therapy

If you, like me, have had your reservations about counselling, please think about it as an option. On our own we can become confused and mired down in self-analysis. To have a trained and skilled person to help you learn the source of your pain and ways to live more healthily is of more benefit that you could imagine. To invest in your personal growth is not as selfish an endeavour as it may at first seem: to know and love oneself is to be able to know and love God and your fellow humans. A broken person breaks others. We will never be fully whole, and never be able to love perfectly before the kingdom of God is fully here. But we can be *more* whole and love *better*. And if we can, shouldn't we aim for that?

There are many kinds of 'talk-therapy' out there, and if you are considering this as an option I would suggest you research these carefully (or get someone you trust to do it if you don't feel up to it). These include, among others, cognitive behavioural therapy, which aims to identify and challenge negative thoughts, while developing more accurate and adaptive thoughts. It often involves doing homework, and takes a lot of hard work, but has been found by many to be an effective form of treatment for depression. Other types of therapy include psychotherapy, grief work and pastoral counselling. When you start trying to track someone down, there are various means of getting help with this. If you are part of a church, you may be able to spend some time with someone on the leadership trained in pastoral counselling, or they could refer you on: our church has a list of people they have sussed out and trust to do a good job: maybe your church will have the same thing. Your family doctor could be another good source of information.

If you are worried that you might get embroiled in an

endless trudge through inner mulch with no result in sight, it will interest you to know that a recent study on the relationship between the number of psychological treatment sessions and the change in self-rated depressive symptoms found that there is not much quantitive difference once you get beyond eight sessions. In other words, only eight sessions can make a real change for the better.[3] This obviously depends on the kind of therapy you are doing (you would need a lot more than eight sessions to get anywhere in psychotherapy), but most have a shelf life and don't go on indefinitely.

Happy Pills

My first prejudice to be challenged was the value of counselling. I was, however, adamant that I would never, ever, be drawn into the whole medication fiasco. I held on for months, brushing off Dr R.'s attempts to convince me of the benefits of certain chemical formulas with the air of someone who has found their position and intends to stay there, thank you. When I finally agreed, I wished I had discovered them years before.

My fears about medication were as follows: they would be a sign of weakness, an admission of a failure to handle things myself; they would make me an emotional robot; I would become dependent on them, addicted in some way; people would judge me. To my fears, I now say this: depression is an illness, a physical, chemical fact, and to treat it chemically is entirely rational, and not a sign of weakness any more than taking aspirin for a headache would be. Antidepressants do not make you a robot – you still experience the normal highs and lows of life, but within healthy limits. If I become dependent on them, so be it. We are dependent on many things in life to keep us working: water, air, sleep, food, shelter. I need my pills to keep me working (for now at least) and I have made my peace with that. If people judge me, it is out of ignorance and prejudice, which I once had too. I can help educate them and if I can't, then I can't. I don't need the approval of all, only God.

Antidepressants have been a part of my healing, and I want to stress that they are only a part. They gave me, and give me still now, the energy and strength to do battle with my demons of history, character, habits, and circumstance, but the point is, there is still a battle to be fought. Dorothy Rowe writes, '...there is no pill which can change the memories of an unhappy childhood into memories of a happy one; or turn an unhappy marriage into a happy one; or fill the person who takes the drugs with a permanent, unshakeable self-confidence...If you have some of the problems that life can bring – and all of you do – then taking a drug which reduces the awareness of pain and fear can bring you periods of respite and help you rest, but such a reduction in awareness cannot solve your problems.'[4]

There are many forms of antidepressants on the market today. It took me four tries to find the one I am on at the moment, and I know others who have gone through even more before getting a good fit. If you have been depressed for a significant length of time, and have other strategies for getting well in place (i.e. you are not hoping for the pills to do all the work) I would recommend that you think seriously about trying medication, and persevere until you find the one that works for you. Bear in mind that the majority take about three weeks to kick in, and that many side effects wear off after the first few days. Side effects you might experience include a dry mouth, urinary retention and sexual dysfunction among others.

Don't come off them the minute you feel better, as it is usually a good idea to take a decent time to stabilise, and never stop them suddenly – it will make you feel dreadful, and can be dangerous. I once forgot to take mine for a few days and felt like my head was floating and spinning above my body: weird and horrible. You'll need to gradually decrease the dosage over several weeks, and it should be done under the supervision of your doctor.

I want to add a cautionary note to this section. It can be a temptation to turn too quickly to medication at the first twinge of discomfort. The danger of this is two-fold as I see it: firstly, pain has a message. It is telling us that something is not right and needs addressing. If we are wise we will listen. The dreadful thing about leprosy is that the nerves are dulled and thus when an injury is caused, say a thorn is embedded in a heel, that person will continue to walk on the thorn until severe damage is caused, rather than leaping into the air with a yelp and then extracting said thorn forthwith.[5] Secondly, we cannot and should not expect a life that is pure comfort. Solomon states with rather brutal insight that, 'people who suppose that bliss is their birthright pop cavalcades of pills in a futile bid to alleviate those mild discomforts that texture every life.'[6] So, by all means take them, but only if you are sure that they are necessary. Lastly, they do not work for everyone. Pregnant women, patients with severe physical disorders and many older people find that they cannot be treated with the appropriate anti-depressant at adequate dosages.

Self-Help

Therapy and medication have made an immense difference to my progress, but they may not be for everyone. You may find it very difficult to find the right person to see: my friend Suzy tried four different counsellors before finally giving up. It can prove expensive and out of your budget. Medication is not effective for everyone, and some people are resistant to ingesting chemicals of any kind so won't go this route out of principle. You may be depressed but not so deeply that you feel it merits the attention of a professional therapist or a visit to the doctor – life is ticking along fine, but you know you are not quite operating at par. You may be stuck out in the 'boondocks' as they say in Canada, far from the resources available in urban areas, and simply not able to access a counsellor or medication. If any of this rings true for you, all is not lost! Many people have successfully got on top of their depression by themselves, through grit, discipline and the help of certain books and techniques. I refer you to the chapter in this book on survival strategies as well as the book recommendations. In England the NHS is struggling to meet the needs of its many clinically depressed citizens – up to 50 per cent of those seen by GPs have symptoms of depression and anxiety[7] – and is pioneering a computer program that takes people through cognitive behavioural therapy in the comfort of their own homes. There are also various organisations and societies that offer help, information and a listening ear, as well as running support groups around the country and online. Among them are Depression Alliance (www.depressionalliance.org), Manic Depression Fellowship (www.mdf.org.uk) and the Fellowship of Depressives Anonymous (www.depressionanon.co.uk). In addition, some of us are blessed with a community of loving, committed and insightful friends, whose care and presence can make the world of difference, and gradually lead us back to health.

Exceptional Healing from the Hand of God

I struggled with what to call this little section, as I believe all healing is from the hand of God, by whatever means. I am referring here to the healing that takes an obvious miraculous form, occurring with no medical intervention of note and as a direct result of prayer. If you believe that God can heal broken bones, kill cancer cells and even restore life to a dead body, which I emphatically do, then God can of course take a broken mind and spirit and mend them. To desire for this to happen and to pray for healing to come in this manner is right and good. There are, however, important qualifications that come along with that statement. First, while we can be assured of being reconciled to God through Christ's death, we have no assurance of physical healing or well-being in this life. Healing does occur here and there, but it is not guaranteed to us. When it happens, it is a sign and symbol of things to come, and a matter for great rejoicing and gratitude. When it doesn't, it is because we are still living in the 'now and not yet', a time and place of brokenness and suffering, in the midst of which, God's presence and love is to be found. Second, I recommend great caution and sensitivity when praying for someone in this way. Please don't make it an issue of the person's faith, because if they are depressed I predict they won't be feeling strong in that department and any added sense of guilt or responsibility is going to make things worse. Third, remember that all healing is from God, including that which comes from the slog of working hard at issues and chemistry, thoughts and behaviour, and that sometimes the process itself is of great spiritual value. An instant result would be gratifying and easy, but maybe isn't always the best thing for the person. As a carer, we may be praying this particular prayer because we (understandably) would rather God step in and take the problem off our hands than have to trek through the valley with our loved one.

A New Me

I have not been depressed for more than a couple of weeks in three years now. I can have an argument with someone, move house, get low on sleep and worry about money without it turning into a general melt-down, which is novel and very nice! I don't quite believe in my stability yet, so I get a bit panicked when I feel down and think I'm falling off the edge of sanity, but each time I don't it's less surprising. I really do think I have become a different, stronger person. The message is: if I can see a change like that in my life, maybe you can too. If I have changed, maybe the person you love who is depressed won't always be that way. There is real hope for healing:

> I am still confident of this:
> I will see the goodness of the Lord
> In the land of the living.
> Wait for the Lord;
> Be strong and take heart
> And wait for the Lord.
>
> Psalm 27:13–14

Chapter 13

Books

I am one of the rare people of my generation to grow up without a TV. I am missing a whole era of pop culture, and can't contribute much to the misty-eyed reminiscences of Zippy and gang, the round window, or Bagpuss, the pink, stripy cat. We did have a black and white telly for a while. One of us children would have to hold the aerial while the others tried to decipher a picture from the snow storm on the screen. Occasionally we would catch the essential details of the first half of *Nightrider*, which was more frustrating than anything, as we'd miss the culmination of the gripping plot. When we lived above a hairdresser for a while, anytime she used the hairdryer it would stop working altogether.

As a result of this dire deprivation, I turned to books for entertainment, and became a veritable bookworm. (Why on earth did I get bullied at school I wonder? A bookworm with strong religious convictions, a bad haircut and no dress sense should have been right in there with the in-crowd!) I gobbled my way through book after book, hungrily devouring anything I could get my hands on – which didn't by the way include *anything* by Enid Blyton, a staple of most children's literary diet, as my mother had studied children's literature for her final dissertation at teacher training college and had been enlightened about her negative stereotyping of foreigners and those with physical disabilities (the baddies always have swarthy skin and a hunchback and/or scar).

I worked part-time in a book shop[1] in Canada to fund my Masters degree, and one of my very favourite things was when someone would come in and ask me to help them find a book. It felt like introducing them to a new friend. Once an Australian girl who was studying at Regent for the summer asked me to kit her out with a whole library – no financial limitations! She had a surf-school and had only just discovered the joy of reading. I rushed around in hyper-mode gathering armfuls of my favourite tomes and she bought the lot. It was probably my greatest moment of power and influence over another person! Ha ha ha – soon the world will be mine!

What I want to do here is introduce to you some of my 'friends' – books that have been a comfort to me, or inspired me, or just been jolly good company in the bleak old journey of depression. If you happen to get hold of one, read it and find it helpful, then I will be extremely pleased! Books can change lives if you read them attentively and with an open heart (and don't forget your critical faculties or you'll get brainwashed).

Books on Depression

I have to confess, I could never actually bring myself to read a book on depression when I was in the thick of it. I was already steeped in it and it was just too much. Well done if you've read mine while you're depressed, by the way! It was while I was researching for this writing project that I came across these gems. Some of them are more meaty and demanding than others, but I think all of them have something important to offer.

Sue Atkinson, Climbing Out of Depression, *Oxford: Lion Publishing, 2005.*
Out of all the books I read on depression for my research, this is the one I think I would manage the best when actually depressed. The author is writing from the inside – she knows what it feels like, and she is patient, gentle and practical in her style. It is organised in short sections, broken up by

illustrations, quotes and lists which I think would make it easier to tackle when low and suffering from a minimal concentration span.

John Ortberg & Siang- Yang Tan, Coping with Depression: The Common Cold of Emotional Life, *Trowbridge: Eagle Publishing Ltd, 2004.*

This is a really thorough, yet manageably short, overview of depression and its treatment. It covers a lot of ground in a concise and informative way, and I imagine could be a really useful starting point if you are new to depression (in yourself or another). The authors identify three elements of depression that all need to be addressed to get better: (a) affect: feelings; (b) behaviour; and (c) cognition: thoughts. They then offer very practical ways to deal with each one.

Dorothy Rowe, Depression: A Way Out of Your Prison, *Hove: Brunner-Routledge, 2003.*

I was given this book by a friend who had been really helped by it. Rowe really knows her stuff – she's a clinical psychologist with years of experience and research under her belt. You feel that you can trust what she says. The metaphor that holds the book together is that of a prison. She talks about how we build our prisons, why we want to stay in them and how we escape if we want to. Her approach is empowering and inspiring.

Peter C. Whybrow, A Mood Apart: A Thinker's Guide To Emotion and Its Disorder, *London: Picador, 1999.*

I thought this book was excellent. As a practicing psychiatrist, Whybrow is well qualified to approach the subject from a scientific standpoint. As a non-scientist I appreciated his clear and readable explanations and plentiful illustrations. Not one to read by the pool on your summer holiday, perhaps, but well worth the effort.

Spiritually Uplifting Books

These are books that have nourished my soul, inspired me to keep going when God's invisibility is an issue, and made me excited about pursuing holiness (yes, these are cracking good books!).

Marva J. Dawn, Keeping the Sabbath Wholly: Ceasing, Resting, Embracing, Fasting, *Grand Rapids: Eerdmans, 1989.*

This book did actually change my life, cheesy as that sounds! Before reading it, I had not given the concept of Sabbath-keeping much thought, other than feeling slightly guilty for shopping on a Sunday. At boarding school we had lessons on a Saturday where they'd give us homework for Monday, so we'd do it on Sunday. The point the book makes is that a day off a week, any day, is vital, not only for our physical, mental and emotional well-being, but as a symbol of acknowledging that God is in charge, not us, and life will go on if we let go of the reins periodically. Now I am fiercely protective of my Sabbath, whenever it falls in the cycle of an irregular working pattern, and have found my life enriched as a result.

Linda Dillow, Calm My Anxious Heart: A Woman's Guide to Finding Contentment, *Colorado Springs: Navpress, 1998.*

I am a natural worrier. I have found this book so helpful in seeking to become 'content in all circumstances'. It is full of stories and anecdotes, which makes it immensely readable, and has a Bible study at the back which I did and found very helpful. It's definitely a book for women though – sorry guys!

Gordon Fee & Douglas Stuart, How to Read the Bible for all Its Worth: A Guide To Understanding the Bible, *Grand Rapids: Zondervan, 1993.*

Reading the Bible always involves interpretation, and this interpretation affects how we apply it to our lives, so it's vital that we do it well. This is a book that will be of inestimable help in that endeavour. It takes the reader through the main genres in the Bible and explains the different approaches to reading each one.

Richard J. Foster, Prayer: Finding the Heart's True Home, *New York: HarperCollins, 1992.*

Most people I know, myself included, feel a bit burdened and guilty when the subject of prayer is raised – we all know we should be praying a lot, and we all feel like we don't. The great thing about this book is that rather than adding to the burden, it makes you feel like you are doing a better job than you thought, and it makes you want to do even better. There are three sections: inward prayer, upward prayer and outward prayer, and each is divided into types of prayer such as 'the prayer of tears', 'meditative prayer' or 'praying the ordinary'. Each time I've read it I have been spurred on to communicate more with God, which can only be a good thing!

Eugene H. Peterson, A Long Obedience in the Same Direction: Discipleship in an Instant Society, *Downers Grove: IVP, 1980.*

Peterson is known primarily for his paraphrase of the Bible, *The Message*, but he is the author of many other books, all of which I can wholeheartedly recommend. He writes with prophetic wisdom and I never fail to feel challenged and inspired by what he writes. *A Long Obedience in the Same Direction* is an exposition of the themes found in the Songs of Ascent, Psalms 120 to 134, including work, community, joy and blessing.

Yummy Fiction

Sometimes when you are depressed, you just need a good story to take you away from your dark thoughts. Escapism is

OK as long as you know you can't escape forever. These are books to take to your favourite chair with a hot chocolate and a blankie. Enjoy!

David James Duncan, The Brothers K, *New York: Bantam Books, 1996.*
This is a wonderful family drama, following the fortunes of the Chance family with originality, humour and poignancy. It is one of the few books that has moved me to actual tears, as well as making me laugh out loud. It has a lot about baseball at the start, but don't let that put you off – it will reward you for persevering.

Graham Greene, The End of The Affair, *London: Penguin Books, 1979.*
Maurice Bendrix, the narrator, tells of his adulterous affair with Sarah Miles and how she left him suddenly and unaccountably. The story follows his attempts to find out why and perhaps reclaim her. It is an intense and unexpected story and I loved it. I hope you will too.

Mark Haddon, The Curious Incident of the Dog in the Night-Time, *London: Red Fox Definitions, 2004.*
Reading this book was like eating chocolate pudding, it was so good! But better for you than chocolate pudding because it's not fattening and it helps you understand how it is to live life with Aspergers Syndrome.

Barbara Kingsolver, The Bean Trees, *New York: HarperCollins, 1988.*
This is heart-warming without being mushy, and redemptive without being simplistic. A story about a girl from Kentucky who acquires a three-year-old American Indian child, Turtle, and how they discover love and belonging. It is far lighter and quirkier than her later works (including the bestselling *Poisonwood Bible*) and makes edifying and cheery reading.

C. S. Lewis, Till We Have Faces, *London: Fount, 1998.*
This is a wonderful story; a reinterpretation of the myth of Cupid and Psyche. Lewis wrote of it as, 'the straight tale of barbarism, the mind of an ugly woman, dark idolatry and pale enlightenment at war with each other and with vision, and the havoc which a vocation, or even a faith, works on human life.'

Books to Broaden Your Horizons

This list is like a buffet table of tit-bits, and I've included it because they are really good reads and deserve a mention. I think that reading them has enriched my mind and expanded my mental landscape.

Raymond J. Albrektson, Living Large: How To Live Well –
Even on a Little, *Colorado Springs: Waterbrook Press, 2000.*
Our friends Joy and Justin gave us this book when we were first married, and we have really been trying to base our finances on its wisdom since. It's not rocket science exactly, but it's very sound and sensible, and most importantly, godly. Essentially, he advises giving some, saving some and living joyfully on what's left, and always living below your means. But there's more to it than that, so you should read it.

Colin Chapman, Whose Promised Land? The Continuing
Crisis Over Israel and Palestine, *Oxford: Lion Publishing,*
2002.
I have always found the conflict in Israel and Palestine completely bewildering and confusing. I read this book to try to sort my mind out about the basics, and found it informative and helpful. Chapman not only gives a history of the conflict and outlines the perspective of both sides, but he delves into the way the Bible has been used, legitimately and illegitimately, to interpret the situation.

William Dalrymple, From the Holy Mountain: A Journey in the Shadow of Byzantium, *London: Flamingo, 1998.*
This is a great travel narrative/history combo, and provides a fascinating insight into Eastern Christianity past and present. If you are spending your extra cash on redecorating your downstairs bathroom instead of on travel, this is a great way to explore from your armchair. Dalrymple is a superb guide and companion for the journey.

Marq De Villiers, The Heartbreak Grape: A Journey in Search of the Perfect Pinot Noir, *Toronto: HarperCollins, 1993.*
I have a story about this book. I picked it up at my local library in West Point Grey because it looked interesting and I thought it would increase my bluffing ability. It was interesting, and it did give me more bluffing fodder, and the chap the story is about, Josh Jensen, reminded me of my dad. So for Christmas that year, I got him a copy of the book and the cheapest bottle of Pinot Noir from the Calera Jensen cellars I could find. Well, it turned out that Dad had sat next to Josh Jensen on a flight between Bangkok and Rangoon in the 70s. He wrote him a letter and they have since had him to stay in France a couple of times and become friends.

Kate Fox, Watching the English: The Hidden Rules of English Behaviour, *London: Hodder & Stoughton, 2004.*
I bought this book because I work with people from Poland, the Philippines, Zimbabwe, Lithuania, India, South Africa and Kenya, and am finding it hard to relate to them all sometimes. I figured the place to start was to try and understand my own culture. *Watching the English* is funny, enlightening and embarrassing, as you see the foibles of your own behaviour in the cold light of an anthropologist's beam.

Dr Catherine Hamlin (with John Little), The Hospital By the River: A Story of Hope, *Oxford: Monarch, 2001.*
This is the story of two Australian doctors who set up a

hospital in Ethiopia for women suffering the damage of obstructed labours. It is 304 pages long but I read it in two days because I was so gripped. It is like sitting at the feet of a wise and godly lady listening to amazing stories. It is full of interesting insights into Ethiopian culture and history, medical progression and the astonishing ability to endure suffering. The lasting impression is that Dr Hamlin has found joy and satisfaction in serving the poorest of the poor, and it is a true inspiration.

Books to Make You Laugh

I have been reading 1 Samuel lately (thought I'd drop that in so you'd know how holy I am) and it is really, truly comic in places: LOL funny.[2] In Chapter 10, you get all the people gathering to anoint Saul as king, but they can't find him, and turns out that 'he has hidden himself among the supplies'(22). What a wimp! Later on, in Chapter 17, there is a classic brotherly bicker. David goes to the battlefield where the Israelites are fighting the Philistines, and his older brother seeing him says, 'I know how conceited you are and how wicked your heart is; you came down only to watch the battle.' And David replies (imagine spotty, grumpy teen here) 'Now what have I done? Can't I even speak?' (28-9) In chapter 21, he's pretending to be mad so King Achish won't kill him, but King Achish isn't impressed: 'Why bring him to me? Am I so short of madmen that you have to bring this fellow here to carry on like this in front of me?' (14–15). In addition to the Bible, may I recommend the following:

Garrison Keiller, Lake Wobegon Days, *London: Faber & Faber, 1999.*
Keiller's humour gathers force as you become accustomed to his dry, laconic style and mischievous slant on life. His character portrayals are affectionate and warm, and the fictional Midwestern US town he creates is enchanting.

Anne Lamott, Operating Instructions: A Journal of My Son's
First Year, *New York: Fawcett Columbine, 1993.*
I did actually laugh until tears came reading this brutally
honest account of early motherhood. In places, it kind of
makes you not want to have a baby, so I only give it to friends
who are already in the middle of it and can't back out.

Donald Miller, Blue Like Jazz: Nonreligious thoughts on
Christian Spirituality, *Nashville: Thomas Nelson Publishers,
2003.*
Christianity Today described Miller as Anne Lamott with
testosterone, so if you get on well with her, you'll probably
like him too. I certainly do. This book is uplifting and funny
and thought provoking, and I hope you'll buy it because I
think it would give you a buzz.

So how's that for starters? There are a million good books
out there to be read – hurrah! They can introduce you to
kindred spirits, fantastical places, edible ideas, and maybe
lighten the dreariness of your struggles just a little, for a
while. I know they have for me.

Depression can lower your motivation and energy, so if
you can't face going out searching for these books but have a
tiny glimmer of interest in any of them, either ask a friend to
get them out of the library for you, or buy them over the
internet. I suggest either www.amazon.com or
www.regentbookstore.com.

Chapter 14

Redemption

Once you're through the woods, it is easy to look back, don a wry expression and say lightly, 'Well, the going was rough but I am glad I went through those scenic woods! I like the bits of branch in my hair and the scratches on my arms and legs make me look tough: which I am, thanks to that extremely useful and meaningful experience.' As Christians, we have the temptation to add a spiritual gloss to our reminiscences. 'Praise the Lord for leading me into the woods. Hallelujah! Glory be for dark, scary places where we can get lost and learn to be better Christians!' Let me say from the outset, I do not believe in tidiness. I do not believe in easy answers and 'everything for the best in this best of all possible worlds'[1] But I do believe in redemption.

Redemption, for me, means the transformation of suffering into something fruitful and oddly beautiful. As humans we are obsessed by the pursuit of beauty, of happiness, of comfort. The strange thing is, it is not always to be found in the obvious places, the five-star hotels, the mountain vistas, the 'dream-job' or the smouldering eyes of a passionate man. Sometimes, this beauty, happiness, comfort, is in the dirtiest slums or the saddest circumstances. This is a total mystery. But it is true. Consider these paradoxes: Londoners after the war looked back with nostalgia at life under enemy bombs, for the community and courage it engendered. Mother Theresa and her sisters of mercy found the face of Jesus in the homeless destitute of Calcutta.

The human suffering possible on this planet is

overwhelming. I recently read the story of a Scottish woman, Lesley Bilinda, married to a Rwandan Tutsi. He was slaughtered in the genocide of 1994, alongside almost a million others. Many were killed by former friends and neighbours. Towards the end of the book, she writes this, 'I was acutely conscious that there would be many questions I would put to God when I joined him in heaven. But I no longer needed to know all the answers; it was enough for me to know that God was in control and that he was bringing the best out of the worst.'[2] There is no sense that she is attempting to whitewash the atrocities or avoid the complexity of what happened: she goes through the very centre of her agony and doubt, and that statement of faith has the quality and value of pure gold. She is not the only one to experience and witness appalling suffering and emerge faith intact. It is the experience of Christians worldwide and throughout history.

All Things?

Paul, in his letter to the Romans, writes 'in all things God works for the good of those who love him.'(8:28) This oft-quoted phrase has been perhaps false comfort to many for whom 'good' equates to somehow coming out on top: whether defeating illness, defying death, or beating poverty. Moreover, when this doesn't happen, faith in God is shaken profoundly. Can we not in fact trust what the Bible says after all? And how could this be applied to depression? Can God work for our good even in depression? As always, it is vital to read the Bible contextually, and Romans 8 is no exception. The line of argument begins, 'I consider that our present sufferings are not worth comparing with the glory that will be revealed in us.' (18) So the sufferings are there, but seen in the light of what is to come: glory. God does not protect us from 'trouble or hardship or persecution or famine or nakedness or danger or sword' (35) – and I could add, depression – but through these things his greater purposes are still worked out, paramount among which is that we be conformed to the likeness of his son, Jesus (29). And in the midst of the worst living nightmare, we are never, *never* separated from his love: 'I am convinced that neither death nor life, neither angels nor demons, neither the present nor the future, nor any powers, neither height nor depth, nor anything else in all creation, will be able to separate us from the love of God that is in Christ Jesus our Lord.' (38–39)

The hope that we have as Christians, in the suffering that is depression, is that while we groan now, with all creation, waiting for the redemption of our bodies (23) we know one day this redemption will come. And in the meanwhile, 'the Spirit helps us in our weakness' (26) praying on our behalf in words that we wouldn't know how to find, and our experiences, horrific as they may be, can all become part of our transformation into godly men and women.

A Question of Perspective

We cannot help but be subjective in how we view our lives. This means that although there may be some objective purpose, or greater meaning to what we are going through, we may not see it until we can look back from a distance. For some, that distance is only going to come post-mortem. Others have a glimpse in the thick of it, where God graciously parts the mist to reveal the full scope of the landscape.

The best illustration I know of perspective comes from *The Silver Chair*, the sixth book of the Narnia chronicles. Jill and Eustace, two children from England, arrive in Narnia and are given the task of finding the lost prince, heir to the throne of the dying King Caspian. They, and their companion Puddleglum the Marsh-wiggle, set off on a treacherous journey, guided by signs given to Jill by Aslan the Lion. One freezing, overcast day, they come across a rocky plain:

> *In order to understand what followed, you must keep on remembering how little they could see. As they drew near the low hill which separated them from the place where the lighted windows had appeared, they had no general view of it at all. It was a question of seeing the next few paces ahead, and even for that, you had to screw up your eyes...*

As they continue on, they begin to realise that the ground is covered in huge trenches, that twist and turn and come to abrupt stops, and strange looking chimneys and cliffs. They do not pay attention, as all they can think about are 'cold hands (and nose and chin and ears) and hot baths and beds'. When finally they come to a castle where they can recover, they are able to see the land they have laboriously traversed:

> *Down below them, spread out like a map, lay the flat hill-top which they had struggled over yesterday afternoon; seen from the castle, it could not be mistaken for anything but the ruins of a gigantic city... To crown all, in large, dark lettering across the centre of the pavement, ran the words UNDER ME.*[3]

Whether we see the writing on the pavement or just horrid trenches to fall into, we can trust that God can and will work for our good through the tough terrain. We can pray that our eyes will be opened to see what he's up to, and we can hold on for dear life to the hope that his purposes are eternal and that he loves us and never will forsake us.

God's Doing?

As I have come some distance from my depression, it has become clear to me that there are ways in which I have been enriched by the experience, hellish as it was. Did God put me through it to gain these 'riches'? I don't know. All good things are from God, but are the bad things too? Dr John Lockley writes, 'However strange it may seem to you, God wants you to go through this depression... You are actually where God wants you to be, even if it is emotionally painful. To put it another way, if God wants you to go through this it would be wrong of you to avoid it, wouldn't it?'[4] Sorry Dr Lockley, but I vehemently disagree with you on that! All I know is that he doesn't let anything go to waste, and it is my job to have eyes that seek out the redemptive aspects of everything I go through, 'In everything that has happened to us over the years God was offering us possibilities of new life and healing, which, though we may have missed them at the time, we can still choose and be brought to life by and healed by all these years later.'[5]

It may be that it is necessary for us to be broken in order for us to hear God. Whether or not he desires or causes our suffering is no simple question, but we can be sure that he can use it for our good – so that through it we grow in holiness and love. The Bible is full of references to pruning as an image of being refined through pain, see for example John 15:2, Hebrews 12:6, 1 Peter 1:7, and 2 Corinthians 7. When the grapes are crushed wine is produced. Oil comes with the crushing of olives. Suffering sometimes results in good fruit. Eugene Peterson writes, 'The hard work of sowing seed in what looks like perfectly empty earth has, as every farmer knows, a time of harvest. All suffering, all pain, all emptiness, all disappointment is seed: sow it in God, he will bring a crop of joy from it.'[6]

Treasures of Darkness

When I look at my episodes of depression, I can find, if I look hard, multiple ways that God has refined my experiences and miraculously brought diamonds from the carbon.

The best thing to emerge from my depression is

compassion for the suffering of others. I have become sensitised to pain, and I am no longer so afraid to draw close to the hurting and stay there. I have noticed that the people who have helped me the most are those who have gone through tough times themselves. There is an intuitive understanding and kindness that is not present as often in those who have had an easy time of it. There is patience and a grace that usually only comes through suffering. As someone who has survived depression, and come out the other side, I can offer hope to those who can't see a light in the tunnel. Henri Nouwen writes this:

> *Since it is [the minister's] task to make visible the first vestiges of liberation for others, he must bind his own wounds carefully in anticipation of the moment when he will be needed. He is called to be the wounded healer, the one who must look after his own wounds but at the same time be prepared to heal the wounds of others... Jesus [made] his own broken body the way to health, to liberation and new life. Thus like Jesus, he who proclaims liberation is called not only to care for his own wounds and the wounds of others, but also to make his wounds into a major source of his healing power.[7]*

How incredible that our wounds, the places we are weak and broken, can become a source of healing for others! In this way, what we have gone through, or are going through is made infinitely valuable. As someone once said to me, nothing is wasted in God's economy. Many people have used negative things that have happened in their own lives as a way of reaching out to others, turning their suffering from a barren wasteland into a garden where others can find safety and comfort. I could illustrate this in many ways, but a small incident that happened last month springs to mind so I'll tell you about it. Shawn and I were at Luton airport checking-in to go to France for Christmas. It was December 23rd, and the flight was full. We finally got to the desk, and as we were putting our bags on the scales, we overheard an exchange at the next desk. It appeared that one of the two men had a letter from the passport agency rather than the passport itself, which had been destroyed in a load of laundry that week. He was not allowed to fly. The other man was sitting behind us on the flight, and we got into conversation. It turned out that they were brothers going to visit their parents for Christmas – the first Christmas they would have had as a family in six years. I asked what his brother was going to do now he couldn't join them and he told me he was going to volunteer at a homeless shelter. To me it spoke powerfully of redemption.

The depression and subsequent recovery has left me with more awareness and gratitude for small pleasures in life. I still have an acute appreciation for waking up without a ball of dread in my stomach. I am able to appreciate things in life that I am sure I would have taken for granted if I hadn't been depressed. It is like the feeling when a migraine finally dissipates – there is a sensation of luxury created by the absence of pain that you would not have realised was a sensation at all were the pain not there in the first place. If you didn't get hungry, food would not be so good. If you weren't tired, bedtime wouldn't be the great treat that it is (do you remember as a kid trying desperately to stay up later? Now I leap into bed with squeals of delight and a hot water bottle at 9.30 p.m. given the chance). I am someone who has plummeted to the depths but I have also hit the heights. I think that capacity for extremes is part of my personal makeup, and part of me would not give that up were I offered an alternative, more stable personality. I know that although I am now not depressed for most of the time, it will always lurk around the edges and quite possibly come to the fore again. This is perhaps the price I pay for living life in multicolour. Andrew Solomon says the following:

It is possible (though for the time being unlikely) that, through chemical manipulation, we might locate, control, and eliminate the brain's circuitry of suffering. I hope we will never do it. To take it away would be to flatten out experience, to impinge on a complexity more valuable that any of its component parts are agonising.[8]

Each time I have gone through a time of depression, come out the other side, and found I have survived, I have gained a little more confidence and strength to face life's coming challenges. I still have moments of quaking in my boots at the very thought of getting depressed again, but mostly I have a quiet knowledge that if it happens, I will get through it as I have before.

Because I am English, and would find it deeply inappropriate and embarrassing to blow my own trumpet, I can't really say that my depression has made me more Christ-like! Certainly, when I am depressed there's not much about me that bears any resemblance at all to Christ as he definitely isn't self-absorbed, grumpy, or bitter! I would say though, that my faith in God has grown stronger not weaker with each year that's passed, and that my experience of his presence in the darkness leaves me in no doubt as to his reality or his love for me.

Heaven

Life for some people is an unremitting nightmare from start to finish. What can we say for them? Is there anything that redeems their experience? I hesitate to answer, because for some questions an answer is an insult, a belittling of an achingly huge, vacuous mystery. In the face of some suffering all there is to do is stand and weep. Depression can, I believe, be a fate almost worse than death. In it there is no light to guide the way, no cosy corners to sit and contemplate. I can write of the treasures I found down this mine because (a) I didn't go to the bottom of the shaft and (b) I am currently above ground. If you can't see any sparkles in the dirty rock face, and have lost your way under the earth, it's OK. It's OK to admit that there is nothing good to be said about it at all.

The only way that some things will ever be made OK is in the final redemption, the coming of heaven to earth, the renewal of all creation and the end of sin and suffering. I close with this vision from Revelation – the great hope to sustain us through the times we weep and hurt and suffer. 'All shall be well, and all manner of things shall be well.'[9] Amen.

Then I saw a new heaven and a new earth, for the first heaven and the first earth had passed away, and there was no longer any sea. I saw the Holy City, the new Jerusalem, coming down out of heaven from God, prepared as a bride beautifully dressed for her husband. And I heard a loud voice from the throne saying, 'Look! God's dwelling place is now among the people, and he will dwell with them. They will be his people, and he will dwell with them. They will be his people, and God himself will be with them and be their God. He will wipe every tear from their eyes. There will be no more death or mourning or crying or pain, for the old order of things has passed away.

Revelation 21:1–4

Notes

Chapter 1

1 Hart, Archibold D., 'Depression', *The Complete Book of Everyday Christianity* ed. Banks & Stevens; Downers Grove IL: IVP, 1997, p. 287.

2 'Understanding Depression': a leaflet produced by Wyeth-Ayerst, Canada inc., 1997.

3 White, John, *The Masks of Melancholy*, Leicester: IVP, 1982.

4 Whybrow, Peter, *A Mood Apart*, London: Picador, 1998, p. XVI.

5 Papolos, D. & J., *Overcoming Depression*, New York: Harper Perennial, 1992.

6 Whybrow, Peter, *A Mood Apart*, London: Picador, 1998, p. 29.

7 White, John, *The Masks of Melancholy*, Leicester: IVP, 1982, pp. 23–25.

8 Wurtzel, Elizabeth, *Prozac Nation*, London: Quartet Books, 1996, p. 30.

Chapter 2

1 Styron, William, 'Darkness Visible', 1990, quoted in Whybrow, Peter, *A Mood Apart*, London: Picador: 1998, p. 21.

2 Eliot, T. S., 'The Cocktail Party', *The Complete Poems and Plays of T. S. Eliot*, London: Faber and Faber, 1969, p. 402.

3 Rowe, Dorothy, *Depression: The Way Out of Your Prison*, New York: Routledge, 2003, pp. 2–3.

4 Solomon, Andrew, *The Noonday Demon*, London: Vintage, 2002, p. 18.

5 Wurtzel, Elizabeth, *Prozac Nation*, London: Quartet Books, 1996, p. 48.

6 Whybrow, Peter, *A Mood Apart*, London: Picador, 1998, p. 146.

Chapter 3

1 Edwards, Virginia, *Depression: What You Really Need to Know*, Robinson 2003, quoted in *Third Way*, May 2005, vol 28, no. 4, p. 13, 'A Necessary Ache', Atkinson, Sue.
2 *Ibid.*
3 Whybrow, Peter, *A Mood Apart*, London: Picador, 1998, p. 95.
4 Cassidy, Sheila, *Sharing the Darkness*, London: Darton, Longman & Todd, 1988, p. 4.
5 Whybrow, Peter, *A Mood Apart*, London: Picador, 1998, pp. 98–99.
6 Williams, Chris: Richards, Paul & Whitton, Ingrid, *I'm Not Supposed to Feel Like This*, London: Hodder & Stoughton, 2002, p. 245.

Chapter 4

1 Garner, James Finn, *Politically Correct Bedtime Stories*, London: Souvenir Press, 1994.
2 Solomon, Andrew, *The Noonday Demon*, London: Vintage, 2002, p. 103.
3 See also Genesis 17:5, 15; 41:45, 2 Kings 23:34; 24:17, Daniel 1:7.
4 Whybrow, Peter, *A Mood Apart*, London: Picador, 1998, p. 96.
5 Atkinson, Sue, *Climbing Out of Depression*, Oxford: Lion, 2005, p. 37.

Chapter Five

1 Cassidy, Sheila, *Sharing the Darkness*, London: Darton, Longman & Todd, 1988, p. 5.
2 *Psychologies Magazine*, March 2006, p. 44.
3 Story found in Piper, John, *Tested by Fire*, Downers Grove: IVP, 2001.
4 Thomas, *Gilbert, William Cowper and the Eighteenth Century*, London: Ivor Nicholson and Watson Ltd, 1935, p. 356.
5 *Ibid*, p. 119.

Chapter Six

1 Miller, Donald, *Blue Like Jazz*, Nashville: Thomas Nelson Publishers, 2003. p. 173.
2 Mason, Mike, *The Mystery of Marriage*, Sisters, Oregon: Multnomah Books, 1985, p. 46.

Chapter Seven

1 The University of British Columbia is situated on an enormous tract of rainforest donated to the Institution, and surrounding it for miles.

2 Whybrow, Peter, *A Mood Apart*, London: Picador, 1998, p. 63.

3 Solomon, Andrew, *The Noonday Demon*, London: Vintage, 2002, p. 283.

4 Altruistic suicide is maybe an exception, such as when a mother gives up her life for her child, or when a weak member of a society dies so as not to take resources from the rest of the group. I am speaking here of suicide that is purely self-motivated, with no thought to a positive contribution to the greater good.

5 Alvarez, A, *The Savage God: A Study of Suicide*, London: Weidenfeld and Nicolson, 1971, p.74.

6 Ed. Atkinson, David J. & Field, David H., *New Dictionary of Christian Ethics and Pastoral Theology*, Leicester & Downers Grove: IVP, 1995, pp. 825–826.

7 White, John, *The Masks of Melancholy*, Leicester: IVP, 1982, p. 146.

Chapter Eight

1 *Time Magazine*, Volume 165, no. 6.

2 Macdonald, George, *The Back of the North Wind*, London & Glasgow: Collins, 1958, p. 118.

Chapter Nine

1 Day, Richard, *The Shadow of the Broad Brim*, Philadelphia: Judson Press, 1934, p. 175.

2 Watson, David, *Fear No Evil*, Wheaton: Harold Shaw Press, 1985, p. 62.

3 Lockley, John, *A Practical Workbook for the Depressed Christian*, Milton Keynes: Authentic Publishing, 2002, p. 15.

4 Peterson, Eugene, *A Long Obedience in the Same Direction*, Downers Grove: IVP, 1980, p. 97.

5 *Ibid.*, p. 92.

6 I know there are Christians who believe that depression is inflicted on people by Satan. Personally, I think that is a tricky stance and leads to some dangerous conclusions, such as that it should only be combated with prayer and not medication or professional counselling. I refer back to my definition of depression in Chapter 1, above.

Chapter Ten

1 Harris, Miranda, 'Community and Our Inheritance' in *Caring for Creation: Biblical and Theological Perspectives*, ed. Tillet, Sarah, Oxford: The Bible Reading Fellowship, 2005, p. 112.
2 Williams, Chris: Richards, Paul & Whitton, Ingrid, *I'm Not Supposed to Feel Like This*, London: Hodder & Stoughton, 2002, p. 236.
3 Bonhoeffer, Dietrich, *Life Together*, San Francisco: HarperSanFrancisco, 1954, pp. 17–21.
4 The Apostles' Creed in *The Book of Common Prayer*, Oxford: OUP, 1969.

Chapter Eleven

1 McCall Smith, Alexander, *In the Company of Cheerful Ladies*, London: Abacus, 2004, p. 205.
2 Solomon, Andrew, *The Noonday Demon*, London: Vintage, 2002, pp. 35-37.
3 Lamott, Anne, *Bird by Bird*, New York: Anchor Books, 1995, p. 193.
4 *Ibid*, p. 181.
5 Whybrow, Peter, *A Mood Apart*, London: Picador, 1998, p. 29.
6 *Ibid*, p. 27.
7 Curtis, Brent & Eldredge, John, *The Sacred Romance*, Nashville: Thomas Nelson Publishers, 1997, p. 91.
8 Taylor, Daniel, *The Healing Power of Stories*, New York: Doubleday, 1996, p. 47.
9 Gardener, John, *On Moral Fiction*, New York: Basic Books, 1978, p. 100.
10 Beuchner, Frederick, *Telling the Truth*, New York: HarperSanFrancisco, 1977, p. 81.
11 Frye, Northrop, *The Great Code*, San Diego: Harcourt Brace & Company, 1982, p. xviii.
12 Miller, Donald, *Blue Like Jazz*, Nashville: Thomas Nelson Publishers, 2003. p. 35.
13 Peterson, Eugene, *Leap Over a Wall*, New York: HarperSanFrancisco, 1977, p. 4.
14 Newbiggin, Lesslie, *The Gospel in a Pluralist Society*, Grand Rapids: Eerdmans, 1989, p. 38.

Chapter Twelve

1 Solomon, Andrew, *The Noonday Demon*, London: Vintage, 2002, p. 30.

2 Rowe, Dorothy, *Depression: The Way Out of Your Prison*, New York: Routledge, 2003, p. 112.

3 Ford, F. *et al*, 2005 'Optimum Number of Sessions for Depression and Anxiety', in *Nursing Times*, vol 101, no. 43, pp. 34–40. The conclusion stated above is only valid for depresson. Anxiety appears to improve with continuing treatment sessions.

4 Rowe, Dorothy, *Depression: The Way Out of Your Prison*, New York: Routledge, 2003, p. 223.

5 Brand, Paul & Yancy, Philip, *Pain: The Gift Nobody Wants*, San Francisco: Harpercollins, 1994.

6 Solomon, Andrew, *The Noonday Demon*, London: Vintage, 2002, p. 26.

7 Freeling, P & Tylee, A, (1992) 'Depression in General Practice', in Paykel, E. S. (ed) *Handbook of Affective Disorders*, Edinburgh: Churchill Livingstone.

Chapter Thirteen

1 This is not any old bookshop, but rather REGENT COLLEGE BOOKSTORE, the best, most well-stocked, intelligently staffed and ethically managed theological bookshop in the whole world. I kid you not. Check them out online at www.regentbookstore.com

2 MSN-ers, chatters and texters use this acronym, I'm told. It stands for 'Laugh Out Loud'. Thought I would include it to make myself seem 'with it', or something.

Chapter Fourteen

1 Voltaire's *Candide* is a scathing satire on the narrow theology that believes all is for the best, in the face of glaring evidence to the contrary: in the book, the Lisbon earthquake, disease, poverty and corruption.

2 Bilinda, Lesley, *The Colour of Darkness: A Personal Story of Tragedy and Hope in Rwanda*, London: Hodder & Stoughton, 1966, pp. 223–224.

3 Lewis, C. S., *The Silver Chair*, New York: HarperCollins, 1953, pp. 97–121.

4 Lockley, John, *A Practical Workbook for the Depressed Christian*,

Milton Keynes: Authentic Publishing, 2002, p. 19.

5 Buechner, Frederick, *Telling Secrets*, New York: HarperSanFrancisco, 1991, p. 33.

6 Peterson, Eugene, *A Long Obedience in the Same Direction*, Downers Grove: IVP, 1980, pp. 95-96.

7 Nouwen, Henri, *The Wounded Healer*, New York: Image Books, 1979, pp. 82–83.

8 Solomon, Andrew, *The Noonday Demon*, London: Vintage, 2002, p. 38.

9 Julian of Norwich, *Revelations of Divine Love*, London: Penguin Classics, 1998, p. 85.